THE JOURNEY HOME

THE JOURNEY HOME
A Walk with Bob Benson

Bob Benson
with
Karen Dean Fry

Beacon Hill Press of Kansas City
Kansas City, Missouri

Copyright 1997
by Beacon Hill Press of Kansas City

ISBN 083-411-6464

Printed in the
United States of America

Cover Design: Paul Franitza
Photo by Sharp Shooters

Library of Congress Cataloging-in-Publication Data
Benson, Bob.
    The journey home : a walk with Bob Benson / Bob Benson
with Karen Dean Fry.
        p.   cm.
    ISBN 0-8341-1646-4 (hardback)
    1. Benson, Bob.   2. Christian life—Nazarene authors.   I. Fry,
Karen Dean.   II. Title.
BX8699.N38B44   1997
287.9'9'092—dc21
[B]   96-39991
                                                                        CIP

10   9   8   7   6   5   4   3   2

CONTENTS

INTRODUCTION

Almost every week I drive east on Briley Parkway past Opryland. When I come to the Gallatin Road exit I can turn right and look into Spring Hill cemetery. From there, I can see the plot where Bob Benson is buried. I often remember the beautiful spring day 10 years ago when Reuben Welch spoke the final words at the graveside, and we lingered there beside the unbelievable. I still like to turn in for a few minutes to pray and remember.

On some Saturdays I go to the wholesale florist and adopt orphan flowers that would be tossed before Monday's new blooms arrive. I take some of the lovelier flowers, tie them with a grosgrain ribbon and lay them on Bob's marker—always with an unspoken apology for not growing them myself.

Despite all this remembering I have come to realize that it never really occurs to me that Bob Benson is *dead.* Bob is present. Bob is relevant. Bob is *alive.* Abel—another great gardener—was described in Hebrews as "he being dead yet speaketh." For me, Bob is a man who keeps on speaking.

The summer after Bob died I was speaking at Northern California camp meeting. Dr. Ted Martin was also preaching. We went for a walk under the giant redwoods. Ted's son had died a few months earlier and, thinking of Bob, I asked him if he ever had the feeling that he knew what his son would say or do in some situation. "Of course," Dr. Ted replied. "We Christians don't communicate with the dead, but we commune with them."

Because Bob is so real for me I am almost surprised

when, in my travels, I meet people who do not remember him because they never heard him speak. They did not hear him tell those incredible stories in that funny little voice. They have not read *Laughter in the Walls* or *Come Share the Being*. They still think a bologna sandwich is just a snack because Bob has not turned it into a sermon for them.

This book is for people who need to hear Bob for the first time. Others of us know that he is the kind of person that we always need to hear for the first time *again*. We look at our families differently when we hear Bob talk about Peg and Robert and Mike and Leigh and Tom and Patrick. He helps us hear the lessons that the trees and plants and flowers are speaking. He invites us to the wonder of the ordinary.

I walked with Bob Benson for one decade of my life. In 1976 I moved to Nashville to work for him as book editor at the Benson Company. In 1986 he moved to heaven. In between, we shared projects and problems, family vacations and business trips, celebrations and surgeries, and at least a million laughs. He and Peggy did not really *need* another friend, but they always made me feel like they needed *me*.

Almost every room in my house holds some reminder of Bob—a book with his scribbled inscription, a photograph from a retreat, a leather portfolio. For years I collected group pictures of men. They hung in my stairwell—the Men in My Life. Bob's contribution was the best—World War I ambulance drivers—dozens of them crowded into one picture. But of the real men in my life, he is not one of a crowd. He is one of a kind.

Bob's words are the most important words in this book. The most important voice is his voice. I hope you will hear that voice—for the first time or *again*. Bob is usually telling us what Jesus has been telling him:

I think Jesus is saying to us, "You're going out to live

life. Don't take too good care of yourself, find some things that count, stick your neck out, spill some blood, spread some love. The sin is not in breaking rules—it's in holding back."

Like the Savior he loved, Bob speaks softly. Listen.

—*Karen Dean Fry*

———◆———

In Kino's head there was a song now. Clear and soft and if he had been able to speak it, he would have called it the song of the family.

—The Pearl
John Steinbeck

———◆———

1

A PLACE CALLED HOME

BOB BENSON WAS A TRAVELING MAN. He was a frequent flyer before you earned points for it. He spoke at retreat centers and camps that were off the map. We teased him that he should write his own "How to See Europe on $5,000 a Day." Wherever the Christian Booksellers' Association held its convention the Benson entourage was there. If you mapped stories, you would find that they were "born" all across the country. There are friends of Bob Benson in every state of the union and around the world.

So why was this vagabond so filled with thoughts of home? Bob Benson's theme was never "The Sights I've Seen." He was always headed home.

Home for Bob Benson was Nashville, Tennessee. He did not move to Nashville to make it in the music business. He was born there, into a family that had walked the streets of Nashville for decades. His mother, Jimmie Lou, had come from Alabama and married John T. Benson Jr. Mr. John T. was a print representative and sold yearbook contracts to schools in several states. Every Sunday night, Ms. Jimmie and the five children would take Bob's dad to the train depot to embark on a week's travels. "Good-bye" was an everyday word for the Bensons.

Note to the reader: The text of this book alternates between Karen Dean Fry's biographical "portraits" of the man who was the real Bob Benson and writings gleaned from Bob Benson's pen. The reader may distinguish Bob's writings by the sections in *italic* typeface.

But "good-bye" has a different meaning for a child who is leaving his family than for the parent who knows the way back home. As a little boy, Bob suffered from severe asthma. To protect him from the infections that could have proved fatal, the Bensons sent Bob to live with a friend in Miami, Florida, for the winter. When cold weather moved in, Bob moved out.

So the yearning for *home* was born in Bob Benson. He was warm and safe in Miami, but he was homesick for Nashville and for the streets around Brush Hill where his brother and sisters would be playing in the snow. He would come home in the spring, but the prospect of having to leave again was always a reality for Bob. Eventually, he left home by choice to attend college and then to set up a new home with his wife, Peggy, but all the yearning that was born in that little boy still lived in the heart of a busy man.

When Bob and Peggy vacationed they seldom bought trinkets or clothes. They were always looking for something for *home.* They were the first people I met who carried small things with them to set around their motel room so it would seem like *home.* Bob ate in fine restaurants on his travels, but nothing tasted as good to him as the *ordinary* meals Peg fixed at home.

All this love for home and the ordinary things of life is mixed into Bob's stories. We hear it in his description of his role as "official manger scene builder":

At our house, we have a lovely Nativity set of wood carvings of the Baby Jesus, Mary, Joseph, the angels, and the shepherds. It also includes some sheep, lambs, horses, cows, calves, ponies, and even a sleeping rooster. Peg and I bought the set when we were browsing through some shops in New Orleans one fall.

We had wanted a crèche in our home for a long time, and we were taken with the beauty of these figures. Peg is really the dec-

12

orator at our house, and she has a knack for displaying things at their best and making places look special. But she agreed to let me set up the manger scene the first season. I must have done a pretty good job because I am now the official manger scene builder. She did request that I hone my skills on the sunporch the first year, but now the scene occupies the central place in our living room.

I have accumulated a box or two of materials that I use along with the carvings. There are some pieces of driftwood I picked up on our various vacations on the coast. I take them out of the box each year like old friends. I know each one of them for its special size and shape and smoothness. I wish that I could ask them questions and hear them answer back. "Where did you begin your journey? What kind of tree were you? What brought you crashing down? How did you get washed up on that lonely stretch of beach? Did you once hold up a little girl's swing or a boy's tree house? Were you part of a house or a boat or a packing box?" For I believe that everything has a story; it has been somewhere, and it is going somewhere.

I also have a collection of stones and rocks. I found them on trips too—in fields and mountain streams and by country roads. They, too, I suspect, could tell me many things if I just knew how to listen to them. Annie Dillard wrote about a man in her neighborhood who spent all his spare time trying to teach a stone to talk. I think about him every year when I take my stones out of the box.

In early December, I get out all these manger things. With the stones, I make a rocky hillside, and with the wood, I build a barn and a stall. I carefully place the manger, the Baby Jesus, Mary, Joseph, and all the rest of the figures (right down to the sleeping rooster on the roof). Then I light the candle, sit down before this scene again, and try to imagine how this holy story could ever have happened at all.

Admittedly, I have gathered up the materials for this scene from lots of places. But always I am impressed to remember that everything needed to make this sacred tableau can be found in *anybody's neighborhood. Sticks and stones, straw and foliage, dogs and cats, neighbors and a virgin girl. All of them can be touched with the meaning that only Christ can bring, meaning that obliterates the lines that separate the divine and the commonplace, meaning that changes a stall into a holy place and a manger into an altar.*

One of the incredible gifts that Bob Benson brings to his readers is a deep appreciation for the ordinary. For Bob, being in his house, in his yard, with his family was *sight-seeing*. And when he teaches us he heightens our delight in everyday things.

We all are aware of how some ordinary thing can become sacramental to us. Some simple pieces of cloth, stitched together in a special way, come to represent our love of liberty and home and are thus worthy of our bared heads and our crossed hearts. A wilted dandelion somehow forever deserves a place tucked away in our Bible because it was delivered in the grubby fist of a four-year-old. In some way, these become magnetic symbols around which our feelings gather.

One of the things I am hearing over and over again is that it is the desire and intent of Jesus to sacramentalize the commonplace—to bring the meaning and purpose that only His life can bring into the ordinary moments and places and happenings of our lives. Probably we are never far away from something that should be reminding us that we are never very far away from Him.

This ability of His to make everything into a sacrament was evident from the very beginning of His life among us.

Men could only describe the things Jesus did as He walked among them as miracles. His mother took Him to a wedding in the very first days of His ministry. She was embarrassed for her friends because the wine ran out, and she turned to Jesus for

14

help. There were six jars sitting beside the door. They were used to hold the water that Jews used to wash their feet and hands—to cleanse themselves ceremonially. They were empty, and Jesus asked the servants to fill them with water. Try to imagine their chagrin when He told them to draw out a pitcher of this bathwater and take it to the master of the feast. Try to imagine their surprise when the master tasted it and wondered why the bridegroom had saved the best wine until last. John said that this was the first of Christ's "miraculous signs."

Another day a blind man stood before Him. Jesus knelt down and spit in the dust. With His finger He stirred the saliva into the dirt. Jesus took the mud, smeared it on the man's eyelids, and told him that if he would wash in the pool of Siloam, his eyes would be healed. The man did as he was told and went back to his village seeing his home for the first time in his life.

This ability to transform the commonplace was even more evident in the events that surrounded Jesus' death. On the eve of His betrayal, Jesus and His disciples celebrated Passover in an upper room. He wanted it to be a sacramental meal, one they would always remember. So He blessed a crust of bread and a cup of wine and shared them with His disciples. From the two most common elements of every Palestinian meal He made His monument.

The reason, of course, was that He wanted symbols that were within the reach of everyone. Nobody was so poor that they did not have bread and wine. The bread might have been as hard as a stone, and the wine might have been bitter and filled with dregs, but it would serve to refresh the body in that land of sparse wells. And both would have been on the table of even the poorest of peasants.

So a supper became a sacrament, a place where the holy life of God happened. Because of that meal we should burst into song. For it is saying to us as loudly as we will let it, "There is life in the touch of Jesus."

If He can take sticks, stones, straw, bathwater, saliva, mud, and the waters of a murky pool; if He can take a crust of bread *and a cup of wine; if, indeed, He can take these things and crown them with all the meaning His life can bring, why can we not see how different our lives would be if we would truly yield them to Him.*

I have come to think of Bob Benson as an apostle of the ordinary. Again and again he reminded us that the truth, the beauty, the mystery we need to nourish our souls is in the commonplace things of our lives. His theology was woven with the words of children, the wonders of nature, mealtimes, gardening—the stuff of all our lives. His words were "Here," "Now," and, above all, "These." These people here at home with you—the ones who know you the best are the ones who will teach you and trust you and test you.

Home for Bob was always a place filled with people. You could not hear him speak without feeling that you knew Peg and the children and all the other folks in Nashville. Home was *home* because they were there. He was a spokesman for family values before the term was popularized.

The value that Bob placed on family and home was not just a creed or an abstract philosophy. He did not just "wish" they could be together or "hope" that they had wonderful memories. He planned that togetherness. He imagined those memories.

———◆———

Bob Benson was a man of enormous depth and commitment to Jesus Christ. Focus on the Family has repeatedly aired Bob's recorded messages on the radio since 1988. The response was always the same—thousands of people writing to ask for tapes and saying how moved they were by his unique message.

I have never heard a better storyteller than Bob Benson. His illustrations were so interesting and so meaningful that people were captivated by his sincerity and quiet manner. When Bob was alive, I remember saying that I didn't think even he realized what an impact he was having on his audiences. That was part of his charm: his self-effacing manner and genuine humility were what made the man the spiritual giant that he was.

—James Dobson

———◆———

2

THE JOURNEY BEGINS

Bob Benson loved the memorable moments—the ones that you planned, the ones that surprised you. He was also a master of the teachable moment and sometimes built his deepest teaching around times when he had failed or fumbled.

His commentary on the Sermon on the Mount included his own personal lapse into worldliness.

I think most of us would acknowledge that we are thoroughly conditioned by the society in which we live. Our hopes, songs, actions, words, and thoughts are constantly bombarded by our culture. One morning last spring I was going across a campground to speak in a retreat service. I think I like morning services best of all and, as well as I knew, my mind was ready and my heart was full. In fact, my heart was so full I was humming a song to myself as I walked along in the bright morning sunshine. You can imagine my chagrin when it dawned on me what this prayed-up, ready-to-preach-on-Christian-devotion-speaker was humming—"Welcome to Millertime." Well, it is a catchy tune, and I guess that's why they wrote it as they did. For the moment, I was caught.

Somehow when the man who was doing the speaking told you that he had hummed a beer commercial or thrown a garbage can lid, you could relate. Because he was willing to see where the truth collided with reality in his life you would be able to let that truth into your heart. And because it was often some experience that you encountered in your everyday life, the truth kept coming back to you.

Probably no story of Bob's does this for me more often than his vest—for the story of his vest is often the story of my life.

Did They Hear My Vest?
I was invited out to a college to speak the other day—
you always want to do your best at a college.
They are such reservoirs of knowledge and erudition—
at least it seems they certainly should be
when one considers how much learning
the freshmen bring with them and
how little the seniors actually take away.
There was also the added disadvantage of
being in my own hometown—
Five hundred miles is about the distance at which I begin
to change into a downright expert on any number of
important topics and subjects.
So I had studied hard—and prayed earnestly—for seriously,
it is a deep challenge to speak to people of that age.
To try to add some direction to them
from out here where I am—
these 30-odd years from commencement.
And to try to do so in a way that will not tarnish
the brightness of their optimism.
It is not a task that I take lightly.
And I put on my best three-piece navy pinstriped suit—
thinking maybe I would at least look like
"a wise man from the east."
And I went out to chapel and spoke.
They were courteous and they listened attentively to me.

The Journey Begins

Afterward I was talking to some students—
I wasn't mobbed or anything like that—
my safety was never endangered.
When someone looked down at my suit and said,
"Well look at that."
And I looked down to see what it was—
only to see that my vest was buttoned wrong.
All the time I had been standing in front of those students
not to mention the faculty and administration
thinking I was looking reasonably important.
And all the time they must have been sitting there thinking
where did they get this guy
who doesn't even know how to button his clothes?
Since it happened—let me try to salvage
a bit of my wounded pride and honor
by philosophizing about it a minute or two.
It is not hard to button your vest wrong, you know—
all you have to do is put the second button in the top hole.
Or else slip the second hole over the top button.
From then on it is easy as falling off a log.
Because the rest will follow along slick as a whistle—
all you have to do is start wrong—
ending wrong will take care of itself.
And do you know how I hear the words of Christ
coming to me these days?
Very simply.
I guess they would have to be for a
54-year-old who hasn't passed buttoning yet.
But I hear Him saying to me
There is just one way to button your vest right.
There is just one place to begin your life.
There will always be a button left over
or an extra hole—
when you start wrong.
But if you begin right,
if you seek first the Kingdom

and His righteousness—
the Father and I will guarantee that the rest will find
their rightful places.
If I could have told them anything that morning—
I mean in a way that it really stayed with them—
I guess it would have been about the place to start.
I don't know if they heard my words that morning.
I just hope they heard my vest.

Again and again Bob Benson used the mishaps of all our lives to teach us deep truth. You can tell your five-year-old who ends ups with one too many buttons this truth. While you are helping her get the top button right, you can remind her how important it is to begin our lives with Jesus.

For Bob Benson, that right beginning was at Ruskin Cave. He could take you there in his stories. He could make you feel the cool damp air of the natural cathedral where he began his walk with Christ.

When I was of junior high school age, there was a group of us at the church who had driven several men and women out of the Sunday School teaching profession. One by one, licking their wounds, they had gladly retreated to the peace and quiet of the couples' class.

We met in an old attic classroom that was furnished with seats taken from Nashville's newly defunct streetcar system. The backs of the seats still moved like they did when the car came to the end of the line. The motorman switched seats, attached the rear power pole, and moved to the other end of the car to make it the front. As soon as the teacher of the junior high class walked to the front of the room, we promptly reversed the seats and left him at the rear of the coach. Finally, my dad was appointed teacher of the class. That act in itself took care of the behavior of one class member. He promptly went to work on the others.

He suggested that one weekend we go to Ruskin Cave in West Tennessee to camp out. There were some old buildings there that were left over from the days when a college was located there. Dad had attended the school for a year or so, and he was anxious to get close to us by taking us through the cave and swimming in Yellow Creek.

The closer the time for us to take the trip came, the less Dad relished going off by himself with that crowd of boys. He invited some of the couples in the church and prevailed on Mom to go along to cook. He persuaded the pastor to come and speak. Ruskin Cave Camp Meeting was born. That camp meeting was only held for a few years, but there are some great memories from those days in a lot of people's hearts.

The old hotel, itself an ancient repository of memories, was dilapidated and without furniture or indoor plumbing. Stoves and refrigerators and beds and about everything else had to be hauled down there for the camp. It must have been a tremendous amount of trouble for Dad, and for Mom as well, who was chief cook and bottle washer. But it wasn't any trouble for me! We held the services in the cave. It was "air conditioned" before anyone knew what air conditioning was.

Over 30 years ago a close friend of mine, Don Irwin, was speaking in the afternoon service. I went forward and knelt in the straw at a old rough bench and dedicated my life to the Lord and to whatever He wanted me to do.

Just outside the cave there was a fountain that just bubbled up all the time with cold, clear water coming out from under that Tennessee limestone hillside. I'm certain that on that hot, dusty August afternoon I got a drink as I went into service and another when I came out. Over the span of those years some wonderful things have happened to me. I have also had some moments of abject discouragement. But the vow I made that afternoon has been lifelong.

In my office I have a collection of Bibles and Testaments on the bottom shelf of my bookcase. All of them together, from the Thompson Chain Reference *edition of the King James Version, through the Phillips, the* Revised Standard Version, The New English Bible, *and the* New International Version, *mark my sporadic journeys with the Word for nearly 40 years. One of the volumes, now tattered with age, is a* Precious Promise Testament *of the King James Authorized Version with the words of Jesus in red.*

I used it in my younger days when I was a new convert and later when I became a student preacher. My first sermon was preached from that little Precious Promise Testament. *In its flyleaf, there is a calendar marking some events that occurred in my teenage years. Each was an event that had deep significance in my life.*

7/15/46 saved Tennessee District Camp Meeting

8/28/46 sanctified Ruskin Camp Meeting

8/24/47 called to preach Ruskin Camp Meeting

8/26/48 first sermon Ruskin Camp Meeting

Each of those notations marks a time at which I heard God speaking to me. I must confess that on each occasion whatever He said came in such a quiet, gentle way that I did not then, and perhaps still don't, fully understand. I only know that they were turning points for me.

On the evening first noted in mid-July of 1946, I do not recall anything that would have even remotely warned me I was going to round a corner that would send me in one direction, however fitfully, for the rest of my life. In all likelihood on that summer night in 1946, Gene Williams, Bill Anderson, and I went out to the Trevecca campus to the Tennessee District camp meeting in the absence of something better to do. It may have been that my dad, who was the song leader for the meeting, had offered to let us take him home after the service and use the Dodge afterward if we would go and sing in the choir. He had a little Chinese proverb that he often quoted, to me in particular, "No singee, no ridee." But I am quite sure that I didn't join the crowd in the tent pitched on the basketball court next to old Hardy Hall that night with the express purpose of "getting saved."

To my recollection, I had never gone forward or made any

24

kind of profession of faith previous to that evening. To this day I cannot remember having even thought about it until the invitation was given that night. Gene had "gotten religion" a Sunday night or so before, and when they sang the invitation song, he asked Bill and me if we would like to go the altar. I remember he said we could all go down together. The three of us went forward that night for prayer.

I don't recall much about kneeling there with the altar workers who alternated between telling the penitents to "let go" and to "hold on." I don't remember what I prayed, and I can't tell you any answers that I heard coming back to me either. For that matter, I couldn't tell you precisely what I heard God say to me at any of the other times that are duly noted in my Precious Promise Testament. *And it is certain that the outline for that first sermon has been long forgotten by both the speaker and the hearers. But I do know it was on those occasions I first began to recognize the calling voice of God in such a way that I responded and obeyed.*

I don't believe that God suddenly decided that He would speak to me in the summer of my 16th year. Rather, long before that night when I "went forward," in ways I cannot even remember and in processes I could not see or even suspect, He had been standing at the door of my heart and knocking so that I might hear and obey His voice.

Bob was always aware of the sovereign activity of God in his life. During my days at the Benson Company he premiered the Lanny Wolfe/Don Marsh musical *Noel, Jesus Is Born.* Bob had written the narrative for the musical and was the narrator for this first presentation. I was singing the solo in the song "Seeking for Me." While we waited together backstage, we talked about our seeking God, and I began to quote Francis Thompson's "The Hound of Heaven."

"I fled Him down the nights and down the days . . ."

By the time we spoke and sang, we were worshiping our seeking God.

Bob had great confidence in the work of God in the lives of other people. He moved among us with no need to pressure or persuade.

I was up for a kind of three-day vacation with Peg a couple of years ago, and we were out on Nantucket—which is about 30 miles off the coast of Cape Cod. My wife is a serious shopper and, even though I am not a shopper, since we were on vacation, in the interest of fellowship and harmony, we were shopping. And they had a lot of souvenir shops that we went through in a hurry. It had once been the whaling capital of the world and they had everything in the shape of a whale—ashtrays, posters, wall plaques, glasses, jars, bottles, watches, charms, bracelets. Whatever you needed, they had one in the shape of a whale marked SOUVENIR OF NANTUCKET on the front and MADE IN JAPAN on the back.

But there was one lovely place we went, a gift shop called the Cross-Eyed Dove. And when we walked in, we knew that this was not just a souvenir shop. Whoever owned this shop had bought and displayed everything with care and love. In the pottery and the sculptures and the paintings and the macramé, there were lovely textures and shapes and colors and sizes and beauty. And you instantly knew that here was someone who had taste and a love for beauty. Fortunately for me, everything there wasn't Peggy's taste.

The owner's name was Robin, and we became acquainted with her. She had worked around the corner in the "whale store" when the opportunity had presented itself to open her own shop. She told her previous employers that she was going to fill her shop with things she loved. And they told her that she would starve to death. "Buy the things you like, and put them in your house. But for the store, buy all the silly, dumb things tourists will buy and sell them to them and then go home to the things

26

that you love." But that wasn't what Robin wanted to do and she didn't.

On our last day there, we were waiting on the ferry and Robin came along from lunch. And we were visiting for the last time. "Tell me again what you do," she said.

"I'm in the religious publishing business."

"I don't believe much in religion."

"Is that right?"

"Yes, I don't think I believe in God."

"Well, I think you do."

"No, I don't."

"But I think that you do."

"Well, why do you say that?"

"Well, maybe you don't believe in God in a personal sense, but you like so many of the things that He does. You know, all the colors and shapes and textures and fibers and wood and clay—all the things you love—come from His hand, for all that came to be was alive with His life. And you may not call on His name yet, but you'd really like Him because you already like so many things about Him."

We were back up there the next summer and were going up the street to her shop when we met her. "Do you remember us?"

"Sure, you're the Bensons, and you're the one who tried to convert me."

"No, I was the one who was trying to tell you that you were already partly converted."

Am I trying to say to you that Robin could accept Christ because she likes pottery or that there is another way to the Father except through Christ? No, I know about redemption and forgiveness and the Cross and the blood and confession and profession. But are you trying to say to me that God is not alive and speaking to Robin in a hundred different ways?

Confidence in an alive and speaking God was the foundation of all that Bob taught and lived. He watched people he loved struggle to respond to the speaking voice of God. He waited in faith that the God who had given him a place to start knew how to bring Robin or anyone to a moment of choice.

When Bob and I would talk about someone who seemed to be losing that struggle, we would often remind each other of C. S. Lewis's insight about the nearness of location and the nearness of approach. Lewis described how a person who is walking toward a mountain village can be standing on the pathway just above the village—so close that he or she can throw a rock to hit the roofs of the houses. But to really be *in* the village the traveler must walk *away* on the path to follow the road into the village. Bob understood that approach can look like distance.

He also understood that the beginning of the journey is only the beginning.

I have come to know that those brief encounters in the life of a teenager were only the beginnings of His message to me. Those experiences, as important as they were in the directing of my life, were more like the start of a dialogue. It was not as if He had now told me what I needed to know and then just hung up the phone on me. He was not finished with His call for me; He was just beginning. And He still does not seem to be through telling me what He would have me know and do and be.

Looking back across the nearly 40 years that have passed since I first responded to the voice I heard, I am aware of coming to places in my life that I never could have imagined. His providences and purposes have steadfastly moved and worked in and around the circumstances of my life. My choices and commitments, sometimes faithful and true, sometimes hazy and weak, have also been ways that His words have been relayed to me. Even now His calling to me is being reshaped and refined. It is as fresh and new as the morning.

My son Tom asked us one night if it is true that God always wants you to do "what you don't want to do the most." I suppose everyone wonders at times if His ways are good ways. Is He really like a shepherd who "leads beside the still waters," or is He some arbitrary crank who has this uncanny way of making pianists play left guard and fullbacks cut paper dolls?

A couple of months ago I was speaking at a retreat in West Tennessee. Tom, Patrick, and I took the pickup truck and our Hondas. The retreat site was only about 20 miles from Ruskin, so after the Saturday morning service we drove over to see the old camp meeting site. We walked over the grounds and got a drink from the fountain, which was still bubbling forth as crystal clear as ever.

We went into the cave and I showed them how we had set up the chairs and benches to make a place for the services. I pointed out the spot where the choir had stood as Dad led the singing. I showed them the place where I knelt when I made that vow. I told them, as best I could, that just as surely as that fountain still gave forth clear, pure water, His grace and goodness flooded and filled my being that morning just as it had so many years before.

We put on our helmets and rode away. As we did, I was praying that I had answered a little bit of Tom's question. Thirty years—and if it had changed at all it only tasted better.

Bob and I were married for 35 years. During that time he was a speaker, a writer, a publisher, and a preacher. He was a husband, a father, a good gardener, and a poor carpenter. He was my friend, my soulmate, and the love of my life.

For 13 of our years together he battled cancer. Then one day the doctor said, "No more miracles. Bob isn't going home."

I prayed, "One more. Maybe just one more miracle." I wanted one more walk on the beach, one more ride through the country, one chance to walk our daughter down the aisle, to play with the grandkids, to hold me in his arms.

But God had another plan for us. For Bob, He gave him peace and rest and total healing. And the doctor was wrong. Bob did go home—to his new home.

—Peggy S. Benson

3

You Made Me What I Am

Long before any of us realized I would ever need it, I took my premarital counseling from Bob and Peggy Benson. More than any other couple besides my parents, they have shaped my idea of what it means to be married. By the time I came to know them, they had been together well over half their lives. I still have difficulty thinking of one of them without the other.

What I learned from them about life together did not come in a series of sessions in a church office. The things I most needed to know, they lived out before me at the house, in our business world, in our times of leisure, and in several hospital rooms.

I learned how different two people could be and still delight in each other. Bob was an introvert who got his energy from solitude. Peggy is an extrovert who gets her energy from being with people. That worked out really well since the mother of five children is seldom by herself. I watched her protect his solitude and saw him relax as she talked to people who would have exhausted him.

I learned that being together is more important than what you do together. Most of the time when I was with them they were doing things that were part of their jobs as publishers or parishioners or parents. Unless they were just fooling me, the most pleasant part of it all was that they were doing it together.

I learned that you can live ordinary days—even ones that are haunted by sickness—with grace and beauty. I saw it with my own eyes!

I learned that a person can have an unshakable confidence in another's faithfulness.

I learned that one person can fully meet the sexual needs of another.

When people discovered that Bob and Peggy had five children they would sometimes ask if they were Catholic. Peggy responded that they were passionate Protestants! He often mumbled when he was speaking, and someone once commented that he had lazy lips. He said that Peg never had complained.

I learned that marriage is worth the trouble.

What I discovered about the human dimensions of marriage I learned by watching Bob and Peggy. I never heard him speak about the "how-tos." When he talked about marriage he gave us a window to see what it means to live in union with Christ.

There is always a faint sadness on wedding days because it is a day of endings as well as a day of beginnings. There are almost always two women on the second row who are weeping. Often, before the ceremony is over, there are two men sitting there helping with the sobbing. But there is also real joy as two people come to pledge their life and love to each other.

Something funny almost always happens at a wedding. Last summer my second son, Michael, married a lovely girl named Gwen. The wedding was held in her church in Colorado Springs. Just as it was time for the candlelighters to come down front, it was discovered that there were no wicks in the graceful brass rods that were to be used to light the altar candles. All of the wedding party was waiting in the vestibule. Mike and I and the best man were ready to enter the sanctuary from the front. Soon there was a frantic search in progress for two long candles that could be substituted as lighters. The lady who was in charge of the ring bearer and the flower girl joined the others in shaking down the church.

The ring bearer and the flower girl soon despaired of waiting and went ahead with the processional. Fortunately, they discovered that they were alone at the altar and returned to join the rest of the group. The incident didn't bother the bride and the groom. Mike and Gwen were well on their way to living happily ever after.

One part of the ceremony that couples often wish to include is the lighting of a candle together. This signifies their oneness. Three candles are placed on the kneeling altar. The large candle in the middle is not lighted. The smaller candles on either side of the center are burning. One symbolizes the bride; the other is for the groom. After the vows have been spoken and the couple is pronounced to be husband and wife, they kneel. When they rise, each takes their small candle and lights the large one.

I understand their reason for doing this. It is symbolic of two people becoming one. But what happens next always amuses me. When the center candle is lighted, the bride and groom blow out the small candles they are holding.

I always want to ask them if they really mean what they are doing. I don't think that I would have married Peggy 25 years ago if I had known that even before the echoes of the vows had faded away, she planned to snuff me out. I hardly think it would have been fair to have had the same intentions for her.

I understand the meaning of the oneness. But the deeper meaning of marriage is that two people become one so that they may each become more than they ever could have been alone.

During the first years of our marriage we were struggling through graduate school and pastoring tiny churches. We had two young sons, and Peg was working part of the time. It was easy to get into rather lively discussions about life in general and ours in particular. Sometimes she spoke so loudly that I even had to raise my voice to be heard.

Sometimes I had to remind her of some of her faults and fail-

ures. This, of course, was always done in order to help. She always ended such family dialogue with the phrase, "You made me what I am." The truth is, that at any point in marriage, you are in some way responsible for what the other partner is becoming. I think husbands and wives have the perfect right to say, "You are making me what I am."

Well, the years have passed and those early pressures are gone. Peg was a wonderful person then, but she is super now. Bright, warm, open—she is like sunshine wherever she goes. She walks through our company and smiles and hugs and talks with everyone. In fact, I wish she would do more smiling and a little less hugging. Her visit is worth $250 for morale alone. I hope no one ever tells her that, because I get her to do it for a free lunch. The thing that bugs me is that now she never says to me, "You made me what I am."

But I think I helped. And I know that because I was able to get that sweet young thing to say "I do" to all those questions, I am more than I ever could have been without her. Her deep, unshaken faith in me and her love, so warmly and openly expressed have made me what I am. Her sparkling eyes have seen in me things that no one else looked deeply enough to see. In real oneness, there is an ever-growing and enriching twoness.

If you were here now, I would sing you a little song we used to sing in Sunday School, called "This Little Light of Mine." The first verse was "This little light of mine, I'm gonna let it shine." We would all hold an imaginary candle real high when we sang it. The second verse was "All around the neighborhood, I'm gonna let it shine." We moved the candle around the neighborhood as we sang. Then we would hold the candle close to our faces and sing, "Won't let Satan 'whoof' it out, I'm gonna let it shine."

When we think of words like commitment and surrender, I am afraid that most us have the idea that one of God's favorite things to do on a rainy afternoon is to figure out ways to "whoof" us out. In reality, He wants to live in union with you so that you will become far more than you ever dreamed you could

*be. He wants you to burn brighter and shine farther and illumi-
nate longer than you ever thought was possible.*

*And our oneness with each other, and our twoness, should
be the same way.*

One of Bob's stories that has helped so many people understand their "oneness" comes from the early days of
their marriage. What he learned from a wedding gift has
become a spiritual treasure for thousands of people.

*During the year when I was a senior in college, I started a
church in the northeast area of Nashville. I was there largely as a
result of someone else's vision, and I really wasn't very effective.*

*We took some walls out of a big house to make a chapel. Peg
and I later moved into the back three rooms for the first "home"
of our married life. I was young and grew discouraged easily.
The people I called on were not particularly interested in coming
over to help me. This lack of interest is no reflection on the
church; later on I was equally inept at selling Fuller brushes
door-to-door.*

*Just down the street from the church was a lovely, old Victo-
rian house. It was the home of a longtime friend of my folks. She
was elderly and alone and was always glad to see the young par-
son knock on her door. I was young and alone, and I was always
glad to see a sympathetic friend. Besides that, I liked the tea and
cookies.*

*One afternoon, shortly after Peg and I were married, Mrs.
Payne gave me four lovely crystal glasses. They were even lovelier because she told me that they were the only four remaining of
the crystal she received for her own wedding some 60 years earlier. They were thin, beautifully shaped, and delicately etched. We
still have them at our house.*

*We decided not to use Mrs. Payne's crystal. As a matter of
fact, we decided not to use ours either. We're saving it for*

"good," whenever that comes. If using crystal is the basis for judging our married life, we haven't had much "good." Of all the things that were given to us some 25 years ago, the crystal is probably the least used. The toaster and the mixer have long since bitten the dust. We could use another linen shower. But the crystal is still there. We just use everyday glasses like you do.

I don't know why, but I like for glasses to match. They're not too expensive, so when I buy Christmas gifts I usually end up with a set of glasses. The last thing I do on Christmas Eve, after Peg has gone to bed and after the bikes are put together, is to take all the old glasses out and stand the new ones in neat, orderly rows.

After a few weeks, the same thing always begins to happen. Someone will empty the peanut butter jar. Someone else will stick it in the dishwasher. Someone else will put the jar on the shelf. At last, it shows up on the dinner table. There it is, thick and ugly, with part of the label still attached. There is no delicate etching. It doesn't match. It's just a big, old ex-peanut butter jar.

We all know that there are some people who seem to have all the natural graces. They know just what to say and when to say it. They move through life with ease and are like a benediction wherever they go. They are like Mrs. Payne's crystal glasses. Some folks are like that. They are better by nature than others are by grace.

Now, I hate to bring this up. Maybe I don't even need to. I'll just mention it.

We all know some folks who are like peanut butter jars. You know, part of the label is hanging on. There's not much grace and beauty about them. They are always blurting out the wrong thing at the wrong time. You would think that by the law of averages they would accidentally say the right thing once in a while. They are the people who say, "I've always liked that blue dress on you," or "I like that suit better than the ones they're wearing these days."

"You are vessels unto honor," Paul writes. The variety of vessels proves that it is not that we are goblets or peanut butter

jars or root beer mugs that matters. The difference proves that the power does not come from us. The power is God's alone.

We are not great because of what we are. We are great because of what we contain. He has made you a "depository of truth." The secret is this: Christ in you.

I know that there are some conceited people around. You run into them on occasion and usually come away wondering what it is they find to be so exciting about themselves. But for every one of the conceited people I meet, I encounter a dozen in whom I sense a deep feeling of failure and inadequacy. I wonder if the conceited folks aren't about the same as the rest of us. They are just so busy bragging that we don't notice that they are bleeding too.

It is here in the midst of a world of fragmented, inadequate, misguided, striving people that I want to remind you again of those two little words about the secret: in you. As you look at yourself and others through these two words, you begin to see a dignity and worth. He put the secret in you. You're something else!

You. You with the big nose. You with the freckles. You with two left feet. You with the bald head. You with the sagging waistline. He put the secret in you and, because He did, you have an inherent greatness about you.

I heard my friend Grady Nutt say something along this line. I'm not certain that he said it first, but then, I'm not certain that his real name is Nutt, either. No matter who said it first, it is true: God don't make no junk.

God in His wisdom decided that urns, tablets, monuments, and shrines were not fit dwelling places for the truth. He did not choose marble, granite, mahogany, or gold. The secret was to be indelibly engraved in the recesses of your heart. The secret brings an inestimable value to you.

What He thinks of you is a reason for you to celebrate. I mean, here is something to celebrate.

I have often thought that we are limited in the number of ways in which we can express our wonder and joy during church or retreats or even privately. I remember the enthusiasm of my kids as they roll down a grassy slope or jump into a pile of leaves *that I am raking. I see our puppy running circles in the yard for no apparent reason except the happiness of being alive or the pleasure of feeling the wind in her face.*

We ought to have a balloon filled with helium to let go of. We need a hat to throw in the air. We need a whistle to whistle or a horn to blow. Some of us are too old to roll down a hill. We would break something if we leaped into a pile of leaves. But couldn't we run around the block or throw a stone or puff a dandelion? What can we do when we want to celebrate our "me-ness"?

Don't just sit there! Do something! Sing, celebrate, rejoice, hop, jump, run, cry, believe, embrace a friend, hug your kid, kiss your spouse, clap your hands. Whatever, whenever, however— somehow celebrate yourself and the fact that He placed the secret within you. Whether you are a peanut butter jar or something else altogether.

Because He does.

The Bensons learned to do all these things. They discovered that the secret was, indeed, in them. Then one day they found themselves face-to-face with a doctor who delivered a devastating diagnosis. He discussed the gravity of Bob's illness and then wrote "18 months" across the chart. He left Bob and Peggy alone to face the fact that one of their candles was going to be snuffed out.

They talked. They cried. And then Bob added a P.S. to the vows they had taken so many years before. "We will live every day for whatever life we have as if it were our last." And they did. Not for 18 months but for the 13 years until Bob died.

When Bob and Peggy were on the road he would usually get up before Peggy and she would always say, "Bob, would you please turn on my curling iron?" During his last illness, when he knew that he was about to die, he reminded her: "I have to go first, Peg. Someone has to turn on your curling iron up there."

———◆———

Sometimes I think that the only thing about me
that is really like my dad
are my hands.
And when my hands ache from landscaping or building,
I remember that Dad would not wear his gloves.
He wanted to feel the soil between his fingers
and grip the wood and the hammer.
Dad also wanted to touch us
and when he did,
it was sometimes with the hurting hands
of a gardener or carpenter.
Now my hands are like his and,
like him, I have chosen
to live and love
without wearing my gloves.

—Tom Benson
Nashville
1996

———◆———

4

LETTING THINGS GROW

In the months following Bob's death there were some places that I could not go. I did not want to eat at the Elliston Soda Shop. That was where Bob always wanted to go to get meat-and-three. Those little booths always fit him better than they did me, anyway.

I especially did not want to go to Davis-Kidd Booksellers. Bob and I often met there. Sometimes we would say, "Let's meet at *the bookstore* and go from there." More often we would "run into each other" because the chances of our both being there were pretty good.

I confessed at Bob's memorial service that we had hatched a grand plan for Davis-Kidd. The plot was necessarily secret but in no way sinister. We had observed over time that some books were in the wrong sections and needed to be relocated. Often we would do subtle rearrangements—like putting a copy of *My Utmost for His Highest* over in the business section. But we finally concluded that we needed to follow a more radical agenda.

We would enter the store not long before closing time dressed like casual consumers. We would do something innocent—like read a few verses from *Where the Sidewalk Ends* or check out the sale table. Then we would go to our respective rest rooms where we would hide until the lights were turned off and the store was locked up for the night. We knew that we risked having to stand on the toilet and crouch down out of sight in case they checked the rest rooms. But, considering the feats we watched on *Mission Impossible,* this seemed like a cinch.

When the coast was clear we would creep into the store. We considered asking Peggy—a much more law-abiding creature than either of us—to be our flashlight holder. But we knew that she would probably tell Barbara who just might tell Tom and then there would be witnesses. Besides, it would be sad for both the children's parents to be in jail at the same time.

There were several phases to our clandestine operation. We called the first one "The Liberation of Madeleine L'Engle." Her books had been exiled to the young adult section, a travesty to children and grown-ups who need to know how to *tesseract.* Frederick Buechner and Annie Dillard had been trapped in the religion section far too long, and we were determined to bring them to a wider audience.

But the grandest plan of all involved the total revamping of the self-help section. This seemingly benign classification, which had begun with Carnegie's *How to Win Friends and Influence People,* seemed to be growing out of control and the titles were sounding more like "How to Skin Friends and Influential People." We decided to relocate the majority of those titles—including our personal favorites, *Muscles in Minutes* and *Thin Thighs in Thirty Days,* to a new section. After much thought we decided to label those shelves "Lies from the Charpits of Hell."

At this point I would be holding the flashlight while Bob accomplished his grand maneuver. He would fill those redeemed self-help shelves with gardening books—dozens of them. For Bob believed that gardening was therapy and theology. He learned a lot of lessons at the top of a hoe. He loved to teach those lessons.

Every now and then I find myself doing something my dad

taught me when I was a kid. It's usually something I vowed I would never do when I grew up and was on my own.

I don't know why I won't go ahead and admit that I am more and more like my dad every day. I guess it is because I would have to acknowledge that he was right about most things. For instance, he not only loved to garden but loved to garden early in the morning. My brother, John T., and I used to argue over who was going to deliver the morning paper route and who was going to the garden with Dad to chop weeds.

Like nearly every other boy in the neighborhood, I had made up my mind that when I had my own home it was going to have a green concrete yard. But this spring I found myself planting a garden. What is worse, I found that I like to get up early in the morning to work in it. And, just like my dad, I began with a thorough research of seed catalogs. I ordered every one I could find advertised. For a while I thought just reading the catalogs would get the gardening out of my system, but it only increased my anticipation of spring. I made out the order and eagerly awaited the arrival of the package like a kid. We were (really, I was) waiting on the box from Burpee like Dad. And while I waited, I read every magazine and book I could find on how to raise vegetables.

Finally, the seeds came and the weather was warm enough to turn the soil and plant my garden. I guess I should say "gardens" because the rabbits and the cutworms quietly devoured the first one while we took a trip with the kids on their spring break. I'm watching this one like a full-time scarecrow. Peg asked if I was going to plant any onions, and I told her I didn't think so because I hate rabbits with bad breath.

But if I never bring anything into the house from the garden for the table, it will still have been worth it because I always come in filled with wonder. Something about a seed has caught my eye and my heart.

I took those tiny seeds, mailed to me in a box from Iowa, and put some of them too deep and some of them too shallow. I'm sure, now, that I planted some of them too thick and I planted some of them too thin. By all odds, I probably planted most of them upside down. They are not marked "This Side Up," you know. But the secret to their life is not written on the outside, it is within them.

External forces like rookie farmers, obese rabbits, and lumberjack cutworms may torment the roots and harass the stalk. But with whatever freedom we allow the poor seed to live its own life, its built-in energies and knowledge never give up. It knows what it is supposed to be doing and it does it. It knows the rules of life and it lives them. It goes about its business of bursting forth in root and stem and fruit. The seed knows that life is not some proper combination of external forces and factors, it springs from within.

The most striking resemblance between Bob's teaching and that of Jesus was the confidence that both of them had in nature's ability to instruct us. Jesus has built truth into all His creation. Bob was faithful to go to nature to teach him what we sometimes miss, because we do not really feel the soil or see the trees.

If I were part of a tree, I don't think I'd want to be the trunk. In the first place, a great part of the trunk is buried in the dirt and mud. The bigger the tree, the more there is way down there where it is dark and dirty. Always, it has to keep spreading out down in the earth in search of moisture and nourishment. And then the branches are not usually very thoughtful and they reach out in every direction as far as they can and they love to swing in the wind. And the more fun they have, the bigger the problems of weight and balance for the poor old trunk. Then there are the obvious hazards of sign hangers with hammers, and romantics with knives, not to mention woodpeckers and lumberjacks.

I think I'd rather be a branch. In the spring, branches burst into delicate buds. They furnish shade for summer picnics. They are ladders for little boys to climb to the skies. Branches blossom and flower to tell us all that there will be more trees. And branches bear fruit—like big, juicy red apples that you can shine on your sleeve and bite into while the juices dribble down your chin. I'd rather be a branch than a trunk.

And Jesus is saying to us all that He will be the trunk and we can be the branches. Can you hear Him saying to you that He will bear you up in the summer's sun, in winter's storm? That He will nourish and water you, that you will only be barren for a season? That you will soon burst forth in leafy foliage, in radiant blossom, and in life-giving fruit? He is saying something very good to us when He says, "My Father is the Gardener, I am the Trunk, and you are the branches."

I know I am an inveterate privilege-looker, but one can hardly fail to see there is also a lot of responsibility here as well. It seems that it goes without saying, but just let me remind you of some things of which His words remind me.

One is that gardeners do not bear fruit. You never saw a gardener with tomatoes hanging down from his or her arms, did you? Gardeners select the field and prepare the soil and plant the seed and chop the weeds and prune the plants. But they don't bear fruit.

And trunks don't bear fruit. They support the weight and seek out the moisture. They hold the branches up to the sunlight. They bear branches, but they don't bear fruit.

Branches bear fruit, and we are the branches. Suddenly, He seems to be saying to us that if there is any fruit borne in the places we are, we will be the bearers. And if we are not fruitful, there won't be any fruit at all. At least, not until He grows some new branches.

In this simple way, He is telling us that we are to be doing what branches are supposed to do. He is talking about our purpose and our place in life.

If you have the feeling that you are the one who is supposed to keep the saints free of weeds, lay down the hoe. That is the gardener's job. The Father is the Gardener. If it seems to you the

*weight of the whole church is resting on you, set it down. The
trunk will take care of that, and Jesus is the Trunk. You are a
branch, and branches bear fruit—fruit that will last.*

*"I am the vine, my Father is the Gardener, and you are the
branches." The branches that live in the Vine will be cultivated
and tended by the Gardener, and they will be nourished and sup-
ported by the Vine.*

And they will bear much fruit.

When I sit down to write I am usually looking inward for
some idea or insight. If I look out the window, it is usually
with a mindless stare. For Bob Benson, looking out the window was a vital part of writing and speaking. One fall we
were speaking at a retreat. As he spoke on the wisdom of
"letting go" he pointed to a tree outside the auditorium and
suddenly we were looking at what he had already noticed.
The tree might look better with leaves. It might feel naked
without them. But winter was coming. It would rain, and
that rain would cling to leaves. When the temperature drops
that rain would freeze and the weight of all those heavy
leaves would break the branches. But the tree *knows* that if it
lost its leaves that God would give it more "come spring."

Suddenly we listeners *knew* that there were things—
and people—that we needed to let go. If we carried the
weight of a job or a child or a friendship into the wrong
season of our lives, we would break. But if we would "let
go," God would give us another green season. We learned
all this from a tree and from a man who took time to look
out windows.

*Looking out the window of my study, I can see in my own back-
yard a parable that speaks to me about life. Sitting dejectedly in
the corner by the garden compost pile is my scarecrow. He is tattered and faded, evidence of his summers of defending our garden*

*from the birds. He used to spend winters in the shed, but last fall
he somehow just didn't get put away. He stayed on the fence until about February, when a windstorm blew him off and into the
cornstalks.*

*When spring came, I dragged him into a corner of the yard
and there he would have stayed, if not for Jason. Jason Runyon
and his sister, Lauren, had come to spend a couple of nights with
us while their parents took the church youth group on a trip to
Canada. Jason had a great time fighting with this ex-protector of
the harvest. He punched him and jumped on him and finally left
him to die out beyond the back sidewalk. After Jason and Lauren
had gone home, I rescued the vanquished warrior from the field of
battle and carried him back to the house.*

*He really deserved a little better treatment. Leigh and I
made him one spring. He was a genuine, life-sized, fully dressed
(from straw hat to shoes) scarecrow. I did the body work. With a
"skin" of fence wire stretched over a "skeleton" of tomato stake
sticks, and some padding here and there made out of some plastic
dry-cleaning bags, he was ready for clothes. Leigh made the head
out of a pillowcase and painted on a handsome face. He was a
scarecrow of above average intelligence, too, because we used the
Wall Street Journal for brains. He was a worthy addition to our
garden and had done his job well.*

*The way his arm used to swing in the breeze that first sum-
mer made him look almost alive. He was so lifelike that people
who passed by would often wave to him thinking it was me sitting on the garden fence. Once when Mike was home for a visit,
he opened the door to the shed and almost jumped out of his skin
when he saw the scarecrow. Even lying out in the yard, where
one of Jason's solid left hooks had knocked him, he looked so real
that Peggy thought I had collapsed on the way to the house.*

*But, of course, he was never alive and never will be. He
couldn't ever get off the fence on his own and take a walk or
dance in the morning sunlight. He couldn't ever sing a song or
write a poem or pull a weed or plant a row or take a bite out of
one of those Tennessee tomatoes.*

47

My scarecrow has the form, but there isn't any substance. No life is there. He is a ragged reminder that we, too, need to have the touch of Christ to become alive. Without Him we are like scarecrows watching over the little patches of ground that have been entrusted to us—sitting on our fences, never knowing what makes beans sprout and corn grow and birds fly and rabbits eat lettuce.

Without Him we would think that the sun rises and sets somewhere around our own little fence corners—never really laughing, never really caring, never really alive.

Sometimes Bob would be teaching a passage of scripture and you would think "What version is he using? I didn't see that truth when I read mine." Perhaps tilling the soil taught him to dig deeper when he came to the scripture. He reaped a rich harvest for us all.

One afternoon Jesus was standing on the prow of a boat that had been tied to the shore. He was telling the people who had gathered at the water's edge about the Father. Over in the distance, perhaps, they could all see a field and, in it, a man sowing seed. But even if there hadn't been a sower in the afternoon sunlight, they could still picture one slowly going back and forth across the field, scattering the seed with the motion of his arm and digging into the bag slung beneath his arm for another handful.

And Jesus continued with His planting:
A sower went out to sow his seed.
And as he sowed some of the seed fell on the path,
where it was trampled on and where
the birds could come and eat it.
Some of the seed fell on the rock and when
it came up it withered and died,
for it had no moisture.

Some of the seed fell in among thistles,
and the thistles grew up with it
and choked it.
Some of the seed fell into good soil and grew
and yielded a hundredfold.

This simple story must have been readily understood by all of those who were listening to Him that day. I know that I have always understood its rather transparent truth and knew just who He was talking about, haven't you?

Well, I didn't know just exactly who He meant by path and rock and thistles, but at least I knew who He was talking about when He spoke of good, rich, deep soil that produced as much as a hundredfold. It is very obvious, to me at least, that He was talking about me. Or was He?

Lately I have been thinking that this is a story about a four-some that consists of me and me and me and me. I'm old Mr. Goodsoil himself, of course, but I also answer to Pathway, Rocky, or Thistles. The parable is all about me. And it is coming to me that I am not a field, I am a farm.

I have some fields that I have cultivated with His help, and they have, and do, bring forth an increase. But across some of the land there are pathways that have been trampled and hardened because I always went the easiest and shortest way. I took those paths over and over. And the commerce of life has gradually worn them down.

And it is not hard for me to remember my dreams and plans at the beginning of many a planting season. I have watched, with excitement and enthusiasm, the tender young shoots springing up out of the ground. But I also recall the tears and frustration that were mine as they wilted and died because there was no depth to my preparation and commitment.

Down across the creek from the field behind the barn, there is a patch of rich ground. It is already plowed and plant-ed. But I suppose it is also filled with the seeds and roots of thorns and thistles and weeds that I have either invited to come or allowed to stay. And in time they will choke out the *life that He wants to bring me in increase. I am not a field, I am a farm.*

    Let me show you a new way to read this story.

A sower goes out to sow
and some seed falls on the path,
some falls on rocks,
some falls among thorns,
and some into good soil.
And the sower goes out to sow.
And some seed falls on the path,
some falls on rocks,
some falls among thorns,
and some into good soil.
And the sower goes out to sow,
and some seed falls on the path,
some falls on the rocks,
some falls among thorns,
and some into good soil.
And the sower goes out to sow . . .

You should read it about 10 times this way until you begin to realize two things.

The first is that the more we become, the more we see our need of becoming. The deeper the roots of life go, the more we are impressed with their shallowness. The more conscious we are of closeness to God, the more we are aware of the distance that separates us from God. And we realize that we are not fields, we are farms.

The second is that always the Sower goes out to sow. Always He comes to us—never tiring, never discouraged that we have far more poor soil than good.

Always He comes, never despairing of seeds that perish.

Of all the truths that Bob tilled from the soil, I believe the deepest one for him was that *the secret was in the seed.* He believed that the secret was in mums and in maples and in me and in you. He saw that truth at his house and in a greenhouse.

There is a wide interest these days in plants, and many books have been written about the green thumb. I even saw a self-help book for people with purple thumbs. People may need the book, but I doubt that the flowers do.

A few years ago I was in Alabama sharing in a spring retreat with the young adults of a Baptist church. On Saturday afternoon we had some free time. One of the couples at the retreat was in the wholesale flower business. They invited me over to see their greenhouses.

Peg and I love flowers. We have green thumbs—pale green, maybe, but green. I like the warm, moist smell of a greenhouse. In fact, I like everything about a greenhouse.

As we toured the greenhouses, John told me about the various plants and flowers. There must have been a dozen buildings filled with plants that were blooming or about to bloom.

The last hothouse that we went to was filled with pots of chrysanthemums that were just beginning to bloom. Before long they would be loading them for the trip to markets in Nashville, where they would be sold for Mother's Day.

My first thought was that I hated to break the news to John and Brenda. But I know that in the southeast, mums don't bloom in the spring. They bloom in the fall. You know that. Everybody knows that. They certainly should have known.

Being an honest man—one who refuses to be confused by the facts—I told them that a greenhouse of blooming chrysanthemums just couldn't be, because mums bloom in the fall.

"Let me tell you a secret," John said. "Mums bloom best when the days grow shorter. That's how they know that the time is right. About the last of August or early in September they seem to punch each other and say, 'Hey, Henrietta, it's time to bloom. The days are getting shorter.'

"When we want mums for spring sale, we plant them early.

They need to be covered with blooms when we take them to market. When it is just about time to ship them, we go around every afternoon and pull the shades down."

I can just see the poor misguided mums saying to each other, "I can't believe the year has gone by so fast. But the days are getting shorter, Henrietta, and it's time to get on with it."

Now I don't exactly know what to think of someone who makes his living tricking chrysanthemums. But I do know that mums have a secret. They don't have a school or a manual for blooming. They just know it's time.

Don't you wish you had the confidence to believe that when your time comes you will just know *and you will burst forth in blossom? Wouldn't you like to think that the psalmist was talking about you when he wrote, "He shall be like a tree . . . that bringeth forth his fruit in his season" (Ps. 1:3)?*

Mums have a secret.

Bob never peddled new spiritual solutions. He did not have a great deal of confidence in the institutions that often fail, because we often fail. But as he worked the soil, he was always tilling his belief that every human being contains the seed of great things.

Early last spring I was planting my garden. It was late on a Thursday evening, and I was leaving the next morning for 10 days of travel and speaking, so I was hurrying to finish before the darkness came. I had run out of sticks to mark the rows and was about to go to the kindling box in the garage and get some more so the beds would be neatly marked and labeled.

Then I suddenly wondered why I needed the labels anyway. By the time I would get back, the plants would be up and I could see where they were growing. From experience, I knew that the rabbits knew which kind of vegetables that they liked. And I sure knew that I knew peas from spinach. And the seeds sure knew what they were. Who needed labels?

So I just covered the seeds with the cool, moist earth and gently patted the beds and said, "Go ahead and sprout. You know what you are. I'll see you in a few days when I get back." And they did, and I did.

I am not sure exactly what all I think we mean when we say that we are made in the image of God. But part of it, I believe, is that the calling voice of God is sounding out in the caves and caverns deep beneath the soil of our souls. And it is by obeying this call that we learn who we truly are and what we can become.

So if I do not seem to hear Him speak from the outside, and if there does not seem to be any message from the sky, then I must listen to the voice that is within me. For that voice, too, is the purposeful, calling voice of God to us.

Not many of us have enough confidence in ourselves to listen to the whispering voice that comes from within. Most of the time, we do not even hear it. But it doesn't matter because we wouldn't trust it. We cannot believe that this inner voice is capable of leading us due north.

We seek advice from friends and professionals, disc jockeys and Dear Abbys. We put out a fleece. We flip coins. We take aptitude tests. We do everything but believe that we could possibly have the answers deep within.

The message of Paul in this place is that the calling indeed comes in the lives of the unlikely and the "foolish." You think you are unlikely; well, you're not. You have difficulty believing that God could do great things in you; well, He wouldn't.

Now if God can take a tiny seed and, in the process of giving it life, endow it with a knowledge of what it is supposed to be; if He can give it the purpose and strength and fruitfulness to not only accomplish it all but perpetuate itself as well; and if He can give it an inner calendar to tell it when all of this is supposed to be done, why is it so hard to believe He has done the same in our hearts?

Since He had done this for tomatoes and thistles and beans

and dandelions, it shouldn't stretch our credibility so much to believe that His image in us. The image inherent in the life He gives to each of us is calling us to be.

The trick is to hear the voice, to believe it, and to trust it.

I don't know if we work in heaven. If we do, we at least get to pick what we do. I think I came to believe this when I figured out that I was not going to get to be a flight attendant in this life. Bob may already be a farmer. A gentleman farmer, to be sure, but he will be growing things. I can't imagine what his flowers will look like with twice the sunlight!

———◆———

It is hard to explain to a four-year-old that the person I am now is because of the things that were important to my parents when I was growing up. As I am still discovering, there are many valuable lessons that I learned from my dad. For example, I consider him a great teacher of unconditional love because he absolutely convinced me that he loved me greatly every moment of my life and that there was nothing in this world that I could do to change this. Hardly a day went by without Dad looking at me and saying, "You know, Leigh, you are so fine." In fact when it came right down to it, Dad was even willing to stray from the truth to give one of us a little support. I distinctly remember the song that he used to sing to me in junior high school. I must preface this by telling you that at that point in my life I had a very small face with very big features, buck teeth, braces, glasses, and hair that looked a lot like I let my little brother Tom cut it. But this is the song Dad sang to me every night with the utmost conviction:

> *She fell in a puddle of pretty.*
> *She fell in a puddle of pretty.*
> *She got it all over she,*
> *From her head to her knee.*
> *She fell in a puddle of pretty.*

And I think I believed even then, as shy and self-conscious as I was, that somewhere deep inside of me I must have been fine and beautiful for Dad to love me so much.

—Leigh Benson Greer

———◆———

5

CHILDREN

Bob Benson loved to watch things grow. Most of all, he loved watching his children grow. Bob was one of five children. He and his wife, Peggy, also had five. The first two were boys, Robert and Michael. The only girl, Leigh, was born next and then Tom and Patrick. You could not hear Bob or read his books without getting to know the kids.

Bob did not usually talk about all of the children. He told about *each* of them. Once he wrote a letter to his infant granddaughter, Katie, in which he described her dad, Michael.

"Your dad is a good man. He is a good husband, and I really believe he will be a good dad. He is thoughtful of others. The other night your mom was going out to dinner with Grandmother Peg and Aunt Leigh and you were staying home with him. They couldn't be gone too long because your mother was taking your dinner with her. While she was getting ready, your daddy pressed her dress. That is like him.

"He has always had a kind heart. He was a collector of stray animals when he was little, and he instantly sided with the underdog in every situation. That is not to say that he does not have his faults. He does have a stubborn streak in him. I think that it came from Peg's side of the family, and she thinks that it

came from mine. There really is enough of it on both sides of the tree to rub off on everyone. I am sure that in 12 or 13 years or so there will be times when you'll stop saying 'Dad' and begin to say 'Dad-dee' with much frustration and consternation on the last syllable. But by then you will love him so much that you will probably forgive him.

"To tell you the truth, dads are usually real dumb about a lot of stuff. I guess because they are dads, everybody, including themselves, expects them to have the answer. So they speak up and look dumber than ever. Your mother can smooth all that over. She'll help you find the right answer and show you a way to preserve your dad's dignity at the same time.

"And your dad is honest. I remember once when he was very small his mother cautioned him against riding his trike in the street. As I recall there was even a mild threat involved. The driveway went up a slight grade into a carport, so it was difficult not to just coast out into the street. After he listened intently to the several warnings given he said to his mother, 'Yes, ma'am, but if I do I'm sorry.'

"I think you'll like your dad."

Bob Benson *liked* his children. He noticed the delightful things about them and was always their very best audience.

My son, Tom, is an avid student of expressions, mannerisms, voice inflections, and all of the other things that make each one of us unique. As a result, he can mimic almost anyone he has been around. And as soon as he goes into one of his impressions, you realize that, although you hadn't noticed it before, that is just exactly the way the person is.

The other night at the supper table he was giving us a little rundown on the faculty at school. Some of them were people that I hadn't met. But later when I did, I knew them. Patrick goes to *the same school, and he knew them and nearly doubled over with laughter watching Tom do his impressions.*

Tom stopped his stories to say that he loved to see Patrick laugh. When we asked him why, he gave us a description and a demonstration of Patrick's face as it moves from seriousness to mirth.

"First, his eyes brighten and his eyebrows widen and then his nostrils quiver and his mouth begins to spread upward and outward at the corners until he passes the point of no return and laughs without control."

In recent days I have lived in the same city as all five of Bob's children. I believe the thing that he would be the most delighted about is their delight in one another, their loyalty to one another. Each of the five embodies some dimension of the man who was Bob Benson.

This year Robert has published a book that takes the honesty and self-revelation that characterized his father's writing to new depths. I sat at an early morning breakfast in Los Angeles and listened to Robert read from his *Between the Dreaming and the Coming True*. In it he describes the mental anguish that brought him to the point of breakdown. The most moving passage for me was when he told of walking into the psychiatric hospital holding his sister's hand.

Michael is a seeker like his father. Leigh is the artist who was Bob. Tom is the master gardener and builder. Patrick is the businessman. They are always checking on each other and celebrating some family member. They know what family means because Bob knew the meaning of family.

The family is just about the place that I want to succeed the most. In fact, I feel that if I fail here, my life will be a failure in spite of everything else that I accomplish, and if I can succeed here, it will somehow atone for all the other failures of my whole life. My most often and fervent prayer is that I will be a successful father.

I love to sing the song that goes, "I have decided to follow Jesus; / No turning back, no turning back." And I like the second verse, "Take this world but give me Jesus, / No turning back, no turning back." But when they come to the last verse, I have to drop out because I cannot sing, "Tho' none go with me, still I will follow; / No turning back, no turning back."

I can't sing it. If I live my life in such a way that I must go by myself, then I think I feel like Moses must have felt when he told the Lord, "If the children don't get to go to Canaan, then blot my name out of the book too."

I was reading somewhere of a retreat for career men and, at the end of the weekend, the last thing each man was to do was to write a headline that he would most like to see in the newspaper about himself. One man wrote, "Henry Smith Was Elected Father of the Year Today—His Wife and Family Were the Judges." But everyone doesn't feel this way. I have actually talked to parents who say that it never occurred to them to tell their children that they loved them. I think that some of the most effective things that I have ever done in retreats and conferences was to send people back home to express love to their kids.

Bob was careful not to set himself up as model for parenting. But he had reasons for the way he treated his children, and he shared those values honestly.

I am a firm believer that the only way to even try to be a parent is with the use of the power of love. We have tried a variety of ways of disciplining our children. When they were small enough, we would give them a quick swat on the rear end. There were times when I felt that all the nerve endings that had to do with hearing, quietness, muscle control, and other vital signs were centered in that general area of the body where they sat down. And I must admit that there were times when I felt that it worked. We used to have a Volkswagen and when things weren't going right in the backseat, you could backhand everybody including Peggy with one stroke of your arm. I was the biggest and they couldn't hit me back, or if they did it was only on the kneecap and didn't hurt too much.

But then they got bigger. I used to wrestle Robert and Mike, and then Mike and I used to wrestle Robert. I try not to wrestle with any of them now. If I wanted to discipline Mike today by paddling him, I would have to say, "Mike, sir, how would you like to bend over so that I can bring you into line?" Because when he is standing up straight he is taller than I am.

When the older boys hit their teens, we tried grounding them once or twice. You know, "You can't leave the yard all weekend except to go to church." I don't know who gets the worst end of that deal—the "groundee" or the "groundor." I just know it doesn't make for much of a weekend with an unhappy boy or two sitting around. And it really doesn't work because if they are old enough and mad enough, they will just leave home.

And you can cut off their allowance, but who needs two dollars a week anyway. So what do you do—ignore them, just keep your head in the newspaper until they get a haircut—what do you do? I believe that the most powerful step you can take is to turn the fervor of your love up another 10 degrees.

It has been my intention as a parent to believe in and respect the specialness of the calling of God in the hearts and lives of my children. I think I can accurately be described as a "nondirective" parent. I'm not sure that this is always necessarily best—and I'm not sure altogether how I came to be this way. Part of the reason is my natural readiness to avoid confrontation if I can. Part of the reason is that I want to believe everything will work out for everybody.

Then, I think, too, that I got caught in the way the generations swing back and forth in their manner of parenting. I re-

member one day when my dad and I were walking along on Church Street in front of Harvey's Department Store in Nashville. I noticed a plaque in the sidewalk that noted the paving had been done in 1927, and I asked Dad if he had walked over this same spot with his father in days gone by. He said he didn't think so. Because he had been the last child in a large family, he had always felt his dad was tired of children by the time he came along. So he didn't remember their walking many places together. Thinking that his father had not been as prominent in his life as he would have liked for him to have been, my dad decided early on that he would get involved in the lives of his children.

For instance, he was an expert at knowing things like where you were supposed to go to college. I didn't have to spend a lot of time deliberating where to pursue my education after high school. Quite simply, I went to the place where he was sending the tuition money. I graduated from high school one night at 8:00 and caught the 10:30 bus. The next morning I was 220 miles away in freshman Greek class at Asbury College. As I said, my dad got involved in the lives and decisions of his children.

Maybe this accounts in some measure for my hanging back and encouraging my five to make up their own minds. One of them will come to me and say, "What should I do about this?" and I will try to look as wise as I can. I will pause significantly, as fathers will do, indicating that I am deep in thought about the matter. Then I make a studied and weighty pronouncement. Most of the time I profoundly answer, "I dunno."

I am not at all convinced that this is a superior way of parenting. Already some of my sons are old enough to look back and point to given moments in their lives when they needed more direction than their father was able or willing to provide. But I have earnestly believed, and tried to get my children to believe, that if they listened to the quiet voice within they would know the answer, because a part of His image within them is His calling voice.

Not too terribly long ago, there were some rumors that Mike was in some trouble. First they came from school and then, of course, they grew more rampant in the fertile soil of the church. And so we called a family council for Peg and me. "What are you going to do about it?" she said.

"Well, what are you going to do about it?" was my reply. "Will we confront him and ask him about it? Will we assume he didn't and treat him like he did? Will we accuse him? Will we subtly tighten the reins of his freedom until he 'cracks' and it becomes evident as to the truth of the rumors?"

Now to be sure, Peg is more of the "Let's get this all out in the open" type and I, through my natural wisdom, intelligence, and cowardice, am generally willing and able to run from all the confrontations, crises, and summit meetings that I can. Unfortunately, this time she chose to defer to me as the leader of the home and turned the matter over to me. With only a couple more questions.

"What are you going to do if it's not true?"

"I'm going to continue to go into his room at night and kneel by his bed and I am going to rub his back for a moment (he sleeps on his stomach) and say, 'Mike, I love you and I am proud to be your dad. I hope you sleep well, and I'll see you in the morning. Good night."

"And what are you going to do if it is true?"

"I'm going to continue to go into his room at night and kneel by his bed and I am going to rub his back for a moment (he sleeps on his stomach) and say, 'Mike, I love you and I am proud to be your dad. I hope you sleep well, and I'll see you in the morning. Good night.'"

It was a couple of months later that he came, first to his Mom, and then later to me, and said, "I was in some trouble at school, but I got it worked out. I'm sorry as I can be, and it won't happen again." And we were doubly proud the day that Mike wrote home from school, "Send me my Bible, I am running for freshman class chaplain." We did, and he was.

I really do believe that steady, patient, unceasing, deep, expressed, oozed love is the only reliable option open to parents. It's better than advice, grounding, cutting the allowance, paddlings, punishments, threats, or any of the other dozens of *dodges and ruses we work on our unsuspecting and awaiting children. Just care, just love, just show it.* Do something.

There have been some times when the temptation as a father has been to assume that it would be best to just go ahead and tell my children what they should do. Still, there was something that kept me from doing this. Maybe it was because I always somehow knew that I could not necessarily know what was right for a given child.

All of your children live in the same house and they ride in the same car and eat the same cereal for breakfast. They sometimes even wear the same hand-me-down tennis shoes. Your children have the same last name and the same parents. But your children are not the same. Not at all. Each one is unique. There are no "boiler plate" clauses that fit all children. They are like snowflakes with their own patterns and their own shapes and their own sizes. They have their own places to land. So their calling must come at precisely the right time and in the right way. They alone can hear the call of the One who can tell them what to be. And just because I am their parent, I cannot make them be tomatoes when they were destined to be radishes. Or scholars if they were meant to be farmers. Or accountants if what they really want is to become poets.

As a parent, I have decided that I can't do or decide or discern everything. But I can live like one who has heard the voice that called him. And I can love. And I can pray. And I can hope. And I can occasionally give advice. I can tell my children that there is a voice that will speak to them.

I can even drop hints. I can remind them (and have) that they could hear the inner voice better if they turned the stereo down, or better still, off altogether. I can say that the most important thing in life is to hear and obey the voice. And I can say that the gravest danger in all of life is to fail to hear and heed the voice.

But I cannot tell them what it will say to them. For the call that is within them is just to them.

Bob believed that the family was a place for celebration.

When I first moved to Nashville I would often stay with Leigh and Tom and Patrick. I would sleep in Bob and Peg's room. My favorite of all the lovely things in that beautiful place was a framed poem that Robert had written for his mom and dad one Christmas.

Most of the celebrations
that I remember well at all
took place in this house.
If we stopped to list them
and celebrate each one over again,
the walls would once again ring and laugh
as they did each time before.
Most of the people I celebrate
still live here.
A list of them is unnecessary
since you celebrate them daily even now.
Most of what I wish
is that the celebrations would continue.
And that I might have a hat always held for me
and a place set even if I'm late
and that my laughter might still
be held within these walls
on certain days.
Most of what I love is you,
though not all,
and I celebrate daily
inside other walls that surround me
that you taught me love and celebration
and helped me go forth to plan my own festivals.

The secret of Bob's celebrations was that they were not celebrating something. They were celebrating *someone*. There were wonderful holidays, but Bob had a way of celebrating the everyday. The soil in which all this thrived was affection—real, nourishing affection.

We have a warm, open, outgoing affection at our house. I really have to give Peggy most of the credit for this. We Bensons were "cool." We loved each other and we knew it, so we didn't have to go around drumming it into each other's ears all the time. Peg's family was a little different in that they celebrated everybody's birthday and Mother's Day and Father's Day and nearly any other day that was half reasonable for celebrating. And Peg brought this warmth to our place. You can't mention something one of the kids did or said without this warm look with the glistening eyes covering her face.

To me our house is the finest place in the world because there is love and warmth and fellowship. Not always harmony, but always love and fellowship. We don't go to bed at night until we have all hugged and kissed and said "I love you" two or three times to each other. And nobody goes away in the morning without getting several "Have a good days" and "I love yous." There are a lot of us, and it takes a while to get it all in, but I think it is the most effective way there is for parents to raise children. Incidentally, it's a very effective way for kids to raise parents too.

We live out a ways from town, 25 miles or so from where I work, and so it is not inconceivable on a busy day for me to leave home before the kids are up and get home after they are asleep. I have lived in my house for four or five days at a stretch and never had a meal with my kids or even seen them awake.

However, I believe so strongly in the power of love that I don't care what time I come in at night or how long they have been asleep, I don't go to bed until I have made my rounds. First I go up into Tom and Patrick's room. Tom sleeps on the top bunk, and I catch his chin and turn his face toward me and look at those blond curls and his fair skin. He's a heavy sleeper and you couldn't wake him if you tried, and he doesn't even know I'm there but I say, "Tom Benson, you rascal, I love you. I thought of you a lot today and every time I did, I smiled."

Then I kneel down by the bottom bunk where Patrick is asleep. Patrick is the baby of the family, and he enjoys every minute of it. I don't know when he is going to grow up, but the way they grow up so fast anyway, I'm not pushing him. I don't care if he takes his teddy bear to college. And he sleeps with any assortment of stuffed animals. If I can reach in and finally find the one that is Patrick, I remind him that I am so very proud to be his father and that I love him very much. He usually says groggily, "Good night," in a kind of "keep moving" tone of voice.

And I cross the hall to Leigh's room and she isn't quite so sound a sleeper. She is a responder, whatever expression of love you say to her will come right back. "You are so fine, Leigh, and I love you," I say, and groggily the pronouns are reversed and I hear "You are fine, too, Daddy, and I love you too." It's always hard to leave such lovely conversation as this.

Then I nearly always stop in a room downstairs where I used to have a study. It's a sad room to me because when you are the oldest and the biggest and you aren't afraid of the dark anymore, you move down there. It's almost a sort of launching pad because when they move down there you know the next move is out to college or to their own apartment or house. But I go down there and "love" across the city to where Robert lives and then across the miles to where Mike is in a crazily jumbled up dormitory room. I say, "I love you, too, and am praying for good days for you."

Why do you do that when they are asleep or far away, you ask? Because of two things. I think that it is part of what it means to share in the very being of God and because I think that it's the noblest and wisest thing I can do as a parent.

And it is doubly effective at our house because Peggy has already made the rounds before me. Between us we want to stuff into the "awares" and the "unawares" of our children as many smiles, songs, kisses, "I love yous," and deeds of love as we possibly can.

One night I bent over and kissed Patrick on the cheek and quickly stood up and started out of the room. I was so tired I thought it was about the last "get up" I had left for the whole *day, when his question stopped me cold and brought me back to his bedside. "Why do you kiss me so fast?"*

Why do we let the finest, most precious moments of our lives go by without a word, thinking that tomorrow or on our vacation, there'll be time to hike and swim and love our children? Why do we withhold from them the very thing they need the most—ourselves and our love?

The time to love is now. The time to begin is right now.

Bob never portrayed his family life as always perfect or peaceful. It was with these people who knew him best that he learned the deepest spiritual lessons of his life.

I know that I could be more holy if it wasn't for certain things that keep going on around my house. All of our bedrooms are on the second floor with the exception of the guest room and half-bath downstairs. Peg and I sleep in one corner, and we have a child at present in each of the other corners.

When you go up the steps you enter a small hall. The first thing you're likely to hear is Patrick playing an album by John Denver. That's not too bad, because I happen to like John, though I don't think his voice will last if he continues to sing that loud. Over in the opposite corner, Leigh is playing Janis Ian. I like Janis, too, and I also understand that she had to sing at the top of her lungs to be heard over John. The thing that makes it hard to adjust to is that son Tom is playing the local headache station over the top of the other two. My kids do not have any hearing defects, but I suspect that with our three phonographs/radios going full blast they soon will.

I just know I could be more saintly if I could have a little more peace and a little less music. I'm convinced that I could move up closer if KDA-FM were not a 24-hour station. Sometimes I think that if I could just ride over the hill on my Honda I could sure be more noble and pure. If I could just get away from it all, I could write poetry and dream dreams and pray prayers. I could make my own music if I needed any. My life would be in union with the great sources of creativity and inspiration. I would be pious and holy. And I would probably be bored and lonely too.

I don't think God especially wants me to be pious and saintly way over on the back of Comer's farm by myself. I think what He would probably really like for me to do most is treat each one of the roomers on my floor with kindness and love mixed with a liberal dose of holiness—even when the music is four decibels above the threshold of pain.

Paul's injunction is to live our lives in the present context of "noise." Fortunately, he did not counsel us to go find a situation where things will be more conducive to being mild-mannered and pious. He doesn't say that when you reach another age and part of your present struggle is over, you can then come around and talk to God. Right now, right where you are—that's where He wants to share your life.

Frankly, there are some places in my life in which it is difficult to believe that He would like to participate. As I am sure you have discovered in my writing (especially since I have tried to tell you), I am a very kind, quiet, mild-mannered, interested, compassionate, loving individual. Except when I'm mad.

There is a scale at my house for registering temper. To my shame, I hold the dubious honor of posting the highest reading ever. All outbursts of anger are measured against my record.

Until the boys got old enough to carry the garbage out, I had to do it. I grew up in a time when the two chief duties of a husband were to bring the money in and carry the garbage out. It was a good day for me when the boys were finally old enough to begin to carry it out and scatter it around on the ground near the cans. They got just enough in the can to entice the neighborhood dogs to turn it over and aid in the distribution process. Such things as pushing the trash down and putting the lid on securely seemed to be taking unfair advantage of the dogs.

I really got tired of picking that stuff up. I was out early one

Saturday morning and I don't remember exactly what happened. Something just got all over me. I don't even remember how the lid got on the roof. I really do think that the can already had that huge dent in it.

But now at my house they say, "Is he mad?"

"Yeah."

"But is he garbage can mad?"

To this day I wish I hadn't done that. It is difficult to see how God would like to be a participant in the life of anybody who acts like that. But He didn't say to me, "Son, when you can get your act together and stop behaving that way and start treating the ones you love the most as if you do and when you can pick up a little garbage without feeling like a first-century martyr and when you can stop raising your voice and throwing garbage can lids on the roof, I might be willing to visit you sometime."

No, it's always the same. I know He would like me to quit acting like that. I certainly hope He is succeeding in the process of remaking me. (A trash compactor has helped some.) But He still desires to come and have union with me. The starting place is in my life.

If the Scripture means what it seems to, He is softly saying, "I want to be a part of your life. I want to be included in the retreats and the good services and the time of honor and accomplishment. And when the garbage is on the ground and the supper is late and the cake fell and the washing machine broke and you took it out on your kids or some other innocent bystander, I want to be there too. When you are pushed and shoved and crowded and you end up striking back. When they call and say it's not working out like you hoped and you're about as frustrated as you can be. When you are just having a good laugh about something and something else comes along and makes you cry and weep. That is where I want to be."

I suppose there has to be a Benson in printing or publishing in Nashville and, right now, I suppose that's me. People say I look the most like my dad of any of us five kids. Mom says I walk like him and talk like him. But these days, as I meet with my clients and play with my kids, I am hoping that I love like him.

—Patrick Benson

Growing up, I remember Bob Benson's words reminding me often that God chose me to love. I did not choose Him. He chose me. It was not hard to imagine Bob as a little boy, standing on the sidelines of any event—eager, expectant, waiting to be included. Even as a man he was slight of frame, his voice frail. And yet, he had discovered the greatest mystery of all. He had been chosen. At great personal cost to God, Bob had been chosen to be loved. And he gently reminded me: so was I.

—Amy Grant

6

THE FINE PRINT

Bob's father, John T. Benson Jr., sold printing for the family business. He represented the company to dozens of schools for whom Benson Printing printed yearbooks. But he was also an entrepreneur, and so he began going to work three hours early every morning to oversee the music publishing company he founded. His sideline would eventually create more revenue than the printing business.

When Bob joined his father at the publishing company, they were selling sheet music and songbooks. Bob started his own sideline. At a trade show he met Bob Mackenzie. Mac is as wired as Bob Benson was laid back. We all said that if Bob Mac stuck his finger in a light socket, it would shock the socket!

The two Bobs shared a vision for the newly emerging Christian recording industry. They worked with the Gaither Trio, Dallas Holm, and other artists. Again, the sideline grew larger than the original enterprise.

Bob Benson was uniquely qualified to work with creative people. He released his employees just as he did his children. And, again and again, they surprised him with their unique ideas and approaches to problems.

The Christian Booksellers Association's annual convention was an important part of the Benson Company year. At one planning session they were discussing the company's participation in the convention. They decided on a concert and someone added,

"Wouldn't it be great to record the concert?"

". . . and for everyone who is at the concert to receive the recording?"

"What if we flew the master back to Nashville and pressed the records so that we could give them out on Friday before everyone goes home?"

"We could call it Beingtogether."

They talked about it. They did it. Because Bob Benson was a man who didn't just make things happen. He *let* things happen.

Another year the company was receiving an unusually high number of customer service complaints, especially about lost or incorrect orders. The "team"—a word Bob Benson loved—produced a slide presentation on the path an order followed through the company. The first shot was of the guy in the mail room. Then came the data entry person and the picker and so on down the line—everyone flashing a Benson Company smile. Finally the order reaches packing and is loaded on the truck. The final shot is of the box falling off the truck as it pulled away from the dock. Even the complainers laughed when the film was shown at CBA.

When Bob talked about business, he was still doing philosophy and theology.

Through my brains and intelligence and brilliance in choosing a father who was in the publishing business, I achieved, by diligence, and hard work, a management position in the company. Since I was not overly trained for this position except through experience, I made a sincere effort to belong to enough management book clubs and take enough magazines like Fortune *and* Nation's Business *and* Business Week *to attempt to formulate some philosophy of management of my own. If nothing else, the books and magazines look very impressive lying around your office. But I have been trying to find out what managers are supposed to do.*

This often puzzles my children too. The young ones ask, "What is it you do? The truck drivers drive the truck, and the wrappers wrap the packages, and the key punchers punch keys, and the typists type, and the artists design and illustrate—but what is it that you do?"

Patrick was supposed to go to work with me one day last fall and I was sick and he got himself a ride and went anyway. I was told later that he tried as best he could to do what he thought it was that I did and he leaned back in my chair and put his feet on the desk and dialed the secretary to order Cokes most of the day.

Somebody I would like has said about businessmen that you are "a feeling human being first and a manager second." Part of what I am supposed to do each day is to walk through the building and know as many of our people as I possibly can by their names and to be able to ask them about their wives and families and dreams as well as why they are not doing their jobs better.

I believe that openness and compassion and love are the best ways to run a business. And because we have a team of younger guys who feel this way, too, I think that our company is a redemptive place to work. We have an old building, and there are times when everybody wants the one old elevator. And it is a growing company, and there are times when everybody wants their job out of the art department next. And there are times when tempers flare and people exchange words they should not have said. They even accuse me from time to time of getting the "tight whites," which means that when I start through the building with my lips tight and drawn, it is time to get in your own area and get on with your job. I'm not saying that it is a perfect place to work, but I am saying that the heartening sign is that when these things happen you will almost invariably find whoever had the "tight whites" retracing his steps in a half-hour or so to apologize.

So I want to say firmly, love is the way to run a business.

What about the bottom line? What about the ratio of the earnings to investment? What are the sales compared to last year? What is the age of the receivables? How often does the inventory turn?

I know there are questions that must be answered, but they are just effects not causes. A business is people—people who create product with other people. Product to be ordered, inventoried, wrapped, shipped, and delivered by people to people who sell to other people.

Bob had an almost unerring eye for beauty and balance, and that gift allowed him to touch dozens of artistic works with his suggestions. He was kind in his response to people's presentations, but he was also accurate in his evaluations. One day a young man came to sing his songs for Bob. He was expecting an audition before a group, but none of the musicians were in the office. So Bob stepped over to my office at Impact Books and asked if I would listen in.

The writer sang. We listened. Bob made a few suggestions. The singer exited, leaving his tape and lead sheets. We were both underwhelmed. Bob looked at me and said, "I hope he doesn't quit his day job."

And like most people who have to deal with profit and loss, Bob knew how the spirit of capitalism could militate against our vocation. He learned a valuable lesson about possessiveness from the family dog.

We have a little dog whose name is Lady. There are times when Woman would have been a better name. She was sold to us as a French poodle, but I have never seen the papers. At any rate, I don't think she is from downtown Paris. She thinks she's a hunting dog. Out where we used to live, she loved to chase squirrels and swim in the lake and catch fish. At the new place, she chases the horses in the adjoining pasture. One of these days she's going to catch one, and then she's going to be in real trouble.

We feed her, of all things, dog food. When our family is going to be away for a few days, we take Lady over to Peg's folks to stay. Now Peg's mother is a real dog lover. She will scramble eggs for Lady's breakfast and fry her a hamburger patty or two for lunch. At dinner she shares her roast beef or chicken with her. She treats Lady royally. When Lady comes home after such elegant dining, she is not excited about the dog food at all. In fact, she refuses to eat it.

Our neighbors have a dog they found at a service station. They felt sorry for him and brought him home to keep him from getting run over. He is not even from rural France. I think his father traveled for a living. They call him, appropriately enough, Exxon.

I learned that the best way to get Lady off her high horse and on to dog food again was to take it out on the porch and offer it to Exxon. You have never seen such looks on a lady's face as we see when she rushes out to greet poor old Exxon. No longer is it a question of whether she wants it or not. It's even deeper than need. It has become a matter of ownership, and Lady is going to own it even if she has to eat it.

And one of the real problems in ownership is that matter of holding on to what we claim to own. The process of gathering up is at the heart of our free enterprise system and as such is respected. We call it hard work, diligence, and Yankee ingenuity. Sometimes, though, our true colors are better revealed in the attitudes and actions surrounding our holding on. What seemed like prudence in possessing really becomes greed in protecting.

There is a deep correlation suggested in these words Jesus prayed, "Father, protect these men you gave me." A simple test that might help us to discern the difference in our motives between prudence and greed would be to measure our willingness to entrust what we have to the Father's watch, care, and protection.

The English word "protect" comes from a Latin word that

means "to cover in front." And we are saying something signifi-cant about ourselves in the things we cover, shield, guard, watch over, maintain, endorse, and support, because we think they are ours.

Part of the image of God in Bob was his love for words and the deep meaning behind them. Much of the creative process in publishing is a matter of refining words and in-tensifying their meanings. This was what Bob Benson could not stop doing.

I was in the music business for 20 years. In all that time I did not write one song. Only a time or two did I even help with one. Phil Johnson, talented young songwriter, producer, and friend at the company, came into my office one morning and wanted me to listen to a new song he had written. It was to be recorded that very afternoon. It was such a lovely idea for a song that I suggested that he hold it for a while to give it time to grow and come to full blossom in his heart and mind. He was gracious enough to accept my suggestion and even asked if I would like to work on it with him. As I recall I wrote a verse and helped some on the chorus. I still believe the things we wrote are true.

He never said you'd only see sunshine,
He never said there'd be no rain,
He only promised a heart full of singing
About the very things that once brought pain.
Give them all, give them all, give them all to Jesus,
Shattered dreams, wounded hearts, and broken toys;
Give them all, give them all, give them all to Jesus,
And He will turn your sorrows into joys.

There are some words that were never never the same for

me after Bob worked on them. The little word "sand" took hold of Bob's mind, and soon he was speaking it into ours.

There is a great old hymn of the church that comes to my mind. It is taken directly from the closing parable of the Sermon on the Mount. If I were before you, I would lift its matchless melody to you.

"The wise man built his house upon the rock, la la la la la la la-la la la. The rains came down and the floods came up, la la la la la la la-la la la."

Then, of course, there is the majestic, climactic second verse about how the storms came and the "house came tumbling down." Actually, this verse was the most fun because in Sunday School class we all collapsed on the floor like the foolish man's house. We don't sing it too much in our church because the pews are too close together.

In a way, it is hard to believe that a random illustration used at the end of a sermon preached on a mountainside nearly 2,000 years ago by an itinerant preacher is really an absolute. That was so long ago and so far away, and in such a vastly different society, that one tends not to even give it much consideration in our complex, technological day.

But the headlines of the newspapers and the quiet tragedies and wounded lives of those you know seem to underscore its truth more than ever. Even the lives that are crashing down in your neighborhood or on your block emphasize again and again that there is just one rock and all the rest is sand.

We like to invent rules and systems and feel there are newer and more practical ways of going about this business of making life work. I came across a paper the other day that I had saved. It was printed in the hand of an eight-year-old. It was a set of rules for the neighborhood club that had been formed to use the lavish facilities of a four-by-eight tree house I had built for the boys. Complete with trapdoor entrance, the house was a perfect place for forming a new society.

The list included the colors for the structure, which has yet to be painted. The roof was to be brown, the outside walls green, the inside walls orange, and the ceiling purple. The color scheme alone was enough to have ended the "new order."

The rules included:

1. No visitors in the clubhouse unless a member is present.
2. Meetings are every Tuesday. (I know for a fact they didn't meet this week.)
3. Dues are 10 cents.
4. Visitor dues are 5 cents.
5. Member may forget dues only three times.
6. A fine will be a quarter.

The officers of the newly formed association tended to follow age order strictly as indicated by: Mike—president; Jay—vice president; Leigh—secretary; Tom—treasurer; Patrick—just a person.

The minutes of that first meeting were duly signed by the secretary, and they are amusing to see and read. I thought of Mike leaving his wife and schooling in Oklahoma City to return each Tuesday for club meetings for the group and of the fact that I remembered that the club never met again after that first meeting. But these future considerations did not rob the situation of a single bit of historical significance when that meeting was in progress.

The real tragedy is that grown-ups also make up little sets of rules and guidelines for life for themselves. Many times they build on premises that are set squarely on sand. They have no more chance of succeeding than a neighborhood club of 6-, 8-, and 10-year-olds. There is just one rock, and everything else is sand.

Consciously or unconsciously, our lives begin to polarize around some area of life. There is the job, the home, the family, the church. These areas do provide parameters for life. They have meaning that keeps us going. But somehow they must be enjoyed with the constant realization that they are sand.

Some things are, of course, thrust upon us. One such thing is work. Like all sand, it makes subtle, unnoticed changes as we go.

Sometimes I think harshly of those who set high goals of financial success and status achievement. It especially bothers me when they are willing to make any sacrifice in terms of time or principle to achieve their stated goals. I don't like the man who told his daughter she didn't know the value of a dollar. I secretly cheered when she reminded him he didn't know the value of a daughter either.

We all know some people whose goals were right. The sand just blew in all around them. They never did say, "I'm going to work such long, hard hours that I'll never get to be with my family. I'll never have enough strength left to do something for somebody else because I intend to invest it all in my business or in getting ahead where I am." They didn't plan to and they didn't mean to, it just happened.

Almost before you know it, the company keeps you running to win a trip to San Francisco or a place in the Millionaires Club or the keys to a new car. And in the process you passed up too many of life's values. The next company banquet is for you, and for 43 years of dedicated service they give you a watch with your name on the back. Everyone says, "We'll never forget you. The old company will never be the same." Monday morning, someone new is doing a better job at your desk. Two months later, someone wonders, "Whatever happened to old what's-his-name?" and you went home with a pocketful of sand. But one has to have a job.

Then, of course, there is the stuff of life. It is a common assumption that riches are some combination of cars, clothes, houses, and various other trappings of the good life. In some ways, though, they are like carrots dangling on a stick in front of a rabbit. We just never seem to catch up.

A $4.00 tie ties better than a $2.00 tie. So we buy one for $6.00 and finance the balance. Then we realize that the $6.00 tie makes the neatest knot and hangs the best, so we buy a $10.00 tie and finance the rest on a three-month pay plan. I don't think God cares what kind of a necktie you wear or whether it has a special little monogram on it to tell everybody you are just a bit better dressed than the average bear. I do think that sometimes the color combination may make Him squint.

I also don't think He is worried about what side of town you live on or how many square feet the house contains. The question, it seems to me, is how much of you does it take to keep juggling all the payments? Is there any of you left when it is over?

My secretary recently told me with pride that she and her husband had bought a new house. I was happy for them. I didn't have the heart to remind her that she had just promised someone that once a month until the year 2006 she would send them a given amount of money. But then we all have to have a house and a car to get to it and a mower for the grass and so on and so on.

It is a well-known and easily demonstrable fact that you can be uncomfortable in a Cadillac and cold in the best suit made. You can be lonely in a crowd. You can be doing very well and still let those down who have the highest hopes for you and your life. You can appear to be a jolly good fellow and yet make your wife and children so miserable that their only solution is to leave you. You can greet the outside world with confidence, while your own heart is so poor and empty you can scarcely force the grin across your face.

And sooner or later, it becomes painfully obvious that real riches aren't always delivered by UPS. They are not necessarily to be found on 200-foot lots. They don't always come with white side-walled tires.

Last September Peg and I celebrated our 25th wedding anniversary. Furthermore, I signed on for another hitch. I remember when we set up housekeeping. I remember how we put everything we owned or had into a 4' x 8' trailer with 3' high rail sides to move to Kansas City to go to seminary. We pulled the trailer with a borrowed car, and Robert lay on a pillow in the backseat. Three years later we had filled the back half of a Bekins van. I haven't the slightest idea what it would take to move us now. Anyone with any notion of giving me a position in another town would probably do well to purchase a truck line first. Little by little, bit by bit, grain by grain, our lives have gained momen-

tum, and we have accumulated more than our share of the relationships, joy, and stuff of life as we went.

Some people have the ability to work their way through all the clutter and stuff and select whiter, purer sand upon which to build. I like to think that I am one of them. I think so because I am a family man. I'm also a scribbler of notes and thoughts on cards, matchbook covers, old envelopes, paper napkins, or whatever. I'm always jotting down a thought, whether it is my thought or a good one. My pockets have to be emptied before anything is sent to the dirty clothes basket or to the stack of stuff that Peg is going to take to the cleaners. One night I laid this profound utterance on a table somewhere: "I'm not the one who makes me happy." The next time I saw the note, Peggy had written, "Who is?" I wrote back so that she would see it, "You and them and Him."

Peggy and the kids have the deepest, richest meaning to me. The warmest, most sacred places in my heart are reserved for them. Most of me and my noblest dreams kneel in worship and thanksgiving before them in the deep recesses of my heart. I think that family relationships are the purest, cleanest, whitest sand of all. It is the sand that has the least trash and is the best place of all to enjoy the sunlight of God's love. But it is sand.

Ten years or so ago, I had had a long, hard week. It was one of those first warm Saturdays of spring, and I spent it in the yard. I was prostrate on the floor feeling my aches, pains, and weariness when Leigh came in. She asked me if I knew what daddies were for. I was so tired I couldn't think of a single reason. She said, "Daddies are for Saturday."

When I got upstairs I dragged out a piece of stationery and made a few notes, which I came across recently. I wrote to myself then that this little five-year-old would soon begin a cycle of puppy love, boyfriends, and going steady that would end with someone asking me, "Who giveth this woman?"

Today is Saturday, and I'm not sure where she is in the cycle at the present. I'm casting my vote for puppy love, but the boyfriend is here. I still remember the shine on her face and the twinkle in her eye when she told me what I was for. I have thought of it a lot. But this is just a temporary stop on her journey. Jesus was trying to say to me as gently as He possibly could that most of what we take for granted is really sand.

I would like to write a book and call it Words I Didn't Use to Like. *The list would include words like "confession," "denial," "cross," and certainly, "rock" and "sand." For a long time, I really wished He had not chosen to call so much of my life that means so much to me "sand."*

The reason the title is . . . Didn't Use to Like *instead of . . .* Don't Like *is that I am beginning to see a little of what it is He was saying to me. Sooner or later I was going to be interested in doing something that mattered. He was gently reminding me of how it could be done. When I got around to it, there is a way to insure the permanence of my accomplishments, and it is by building on His teaching.*

In His parable, Jesus tells us very plainly and pointedly what is the rock. The rock is His teaching. The wise man is the man who builds his house upon the rock, His teachings, His word, His principles.

It does not say directly what the sand is. But He did say that there are only two places where one may build his or her life. One of them is safe and the other is not. The safe place is the rock. The reasonable conclusion, then, is that if there is only one rock and it is the Word of God, the sand is anything that is not the rock.

There is just one safe place. There is only one place of permanence. There is only one sure way to make the things you accomplish last. Anything else, and everything else, is sand.

"Chosen" was a word that Bob loved and lived. He gave it to all of us—refined and polished and taken to a whole new level.

I have come to the place where I dread to travel. When I know that I am going to be leaving home on Friday morning, I start getting homesick on Wednesday. On Thursday night Peg always asks if I am going to pack my suitcase before I go to bed. But just in case the thing is canceled and I will not have to go, I wait until I get up on Friday to pack.

And Peggy will say to me, "Why are you going?"

"Well, I told them that I would come, so I guess I will."

"Why did you tell them that you would come?"

"Because I was chosen."

In recent days it seems so very obvious that I have not only been chosen but also protected and spared. We were playing the little "Why are you going?" game one night not too long ago, and Peggy said, "You have to go."

"Why do I have to go?"

"You were chosen."

Now I know that I am an improbable choice. You certainly cannot tell why I was chosen by observing me. And if you use me as an example, it will be clear that the process by which God chooses men cannot be understood by looking at the choosee.

In the first place, I have consistently managed to be smaller than my contemporaries. One hundred forty-five pounds or so looks as if it is going to be it. And it is stretched over a frame that seems to be going from 5'10¾" back to 5'10". I did get up to 163 pounds once. But I looked like a squirrel with acorns in its jaws. After my recent illness, Tom looked at my legs as I came out of the shower and called me Olive Oyl. In heaven, if I could be about 6'2" and weigh around 235, I would be willing to let someone else have my wings and I'd probably throw in my harp to boot.

I was always a frail kid. I can remember when we used to go out to recess in grammar school. The two biggest and strongest kids in the class were always made captains of the softball teams. Usually they made themselves pitchers of the teams first, and then they picked the rest. One by one each kid was chosen—for athletic prowess, for friendship, for size—until everybody was on a team. Well, almost everybody.

"The game can't start until someone takes Bob," the teacher would insist.

And one of the captains would kick the dust and say in disgust, "We'll take him."

And I was usually sent to play behind the right fielder. I don't think I came up to bat until I was in the eighth grade. I wasn't too surprised to strike out then.

So, I likes to be chose.

In addition to not being very big, I have a very, very soft speaking voice. And a most disconcerting habit of lowering my voice even further when I get to something that I really want to emphasize. People often come up when I finish speaking and say to me, "I couldn't hear more than about half of what you said tonight."

"If you tell me the half you heard, I'll tell you the other half again," is my reply, and it usually turns out they can't even remember the half they heard.

I think of Moses who, incidentally, probably didn't talk loud. He was instructed by God to turn aside and see the burning bush. God did not tell him to scream and jump over the bush. He told him to take off his shoes because he was on holy ground. Holy ground makes me quieter than ever.

It is fun to observe people when I am first introduced and begin to speak. It seems that they are saying to themselves, "Well, I can hardly hear him, so I will try to read his lips." And then they notice that I do not move my lips very much either. When you don't talk any louder than I do, you don't have to move your mouth very much. The words just sort of sneak out. My speech teacher told me that I had lazy lips.

Further, I am a shy person who does not initiate conversations with strangers. I am not even noted for talking to those I do know. If you rode from here to Tallahassee beside me on a bus, I probably would not say much more than "Good morning" unless you happened to be sitting on my hat. To say the very least, I am not noted as a brilliant conversationalist.

If you add it all up, and it doesn't take long, I'm not the most impressive speaker you've ever seen. The other day some-

body was saying, "Where is the speaker?" I didn't mind that too much because it was before the service. It happened again a little bit later, and this time it was more humbling. Because this time I had just finished speaking.

And when you think of a rather shy little man with a quiet voice and lazy lips climbing on a plane to travel across the country to get up in front of a group of total strangers to talk to them, it does seem far-fetched.

So, I understand easily why it appears that I am both an implausible and illogical choice. I can only say that if it seems that way to those who know only a little about me, think how much more it is to me knowing all that I know about me. Fortunately my being chosen does not grow out of me. I am just a choosee.

The answer must be found in the heart of the Chooser. *It was not something in me that made Him call me. It was something in Him. It began in His love for me. And that is why these words of Jesus have such a lovely sound. "You did not choose me. I chose you."*

It was not that I came upon Jesus Christ and, when I saw Him, something within me ran out to meet Him and, holding on to Him, begged Him to lift me out of myself and make me the person of my dreams. It was that He came upon me. His heart rushed out to me. He held on to me. He said He would make me the person that I wanted to be. He saw me. He loved me and chose me. I didn't find Him. He found me.

I heard a story the other day about being chosen. Someone asked another person if he would help him out on a project. He responded yes.

"I think it is only fair that I tell you that you were my second choice," replied the first, maybe with more honesty than was called for.

"Well, that's all right," the willing worker said, "but just out of curiosity, who was your first choice?"

"Anybody," was the reply.

But I wasn't chosen as a replacement for someone who didn't want to serve. I wasn't asked to play in the field someone was al-

ready covering. He saw me. He called me. He selected me. He picked me. He singled me out. He decided on me. He opted for me. He fixed upon me. He determined in favor of me. He preferred me. He espoused me. He chose me.

He did not refuse me. He did not reject me. He did not repudiate me. He did not spurn me. He did not dismiss me. He did not exclude me. He did not ignore, disregard, cast away, throw aside, or leave me out. He chose me.

It was not obligatory, mandatory, required, called for, deserved, necessary, imperative, compulsory, or forced. He just chose me.

It was His open, voluntary, willful, selective, deliberate, intentional choice. He chose me.

Out of His devotion, fondness, adoration, tenderness, affection, attachment, emotion, sympathy, empathy, and love, He just chose me.

And that has made all the difference in my life.

———◆———

In a world of deaf mutes, he was our ears.

When we were blind to the simplest things, he was our eyes.

When we reenacted Babel with our loud disagreements and petty differences, he spoke softly.

And somehow the gentle truth of what he whispered rose above the din to call us back to love again.

He was a hearer; he was a seer; he was a poet.

—Gloria Gaither
From her funeral tribute
March 22, 1986

———◆———

7

READING DEEP

Before Bob Benson was a publisher he was a pastor. He was a seminary graduate and had been trained in theology and Bible study methods. All that knowledge was at his disposal, but he wanted *more*.

I once heard a missionary tell a very moving story about an African man to whom he had given a copy of the Bible. The African was so grateful for the gift, and so profuse in his thanks, that the missionary was puzzled a few months later when they met again. For the Bible was battered and torn, and it looked as though many of the pages were missing. "I thought you would have taken better care of the Bible I gave you," he remarked. "I assumed you wanted it and would treasure it."

And the African man replied, "It is the finest gift I ever received. It is such a wonderful book that I gave a page to my father and a page to my mother and then I gave a page to everyone in the village."

Some years later, I read about a book titled The Joys of Super Slow Reading. *In the book there is an account of a man who was imprisoned during World War II. He was only able to take a single book along with him when he was captured. Since he did not know how long it was going to be before he was rescued, he determined he would make that one book last. And he rationed out its words and pages to himself.*

I certainly believe in the programs that encourage and aid us to read the Bible through in a year. My only misgivings surface through my usual flounderings in the doldrums of Deuteronomy in mid-March. But I also believe there is great value in centering oneself in a given place in the Word and lingering there until it has had time to make an indelible impression on one's life.

It might be a good exercise for each of us to take some small portion of Scripture and, instead of approaching it with the idea of finishing it quickly, try to see how long we could make it last.

It probably would do us all good, we who have so many Bibles in so many translations, to have only a page for a while. Until we had learned it, until we had loved it, until it was ours in truth.

There is a song that comes to my mind when I think of Bob's thirst for a deep drink from the word of God.

> *More about Jesus in His Word,*
> *Holding communion with my Lord,*
> *Hearing His voice in ev'ry line,*
> *Making each faithful saying mine.*

When I realize now that I can express in as few as seven words that deep foundational truth of my life, I wonder what I am doing writing another book. Why don't I just put out a new bumper sticker or get the government to issue a new postage stamp with my message emblazoned on it? When I tell people in the first service of a retreat or conference that I can express all I really need to say to them in a single sentence, I can almost hear them thinking, "Well, why don't you just go ahead and say it and get it over with and then we can go out and play golf or go shopping?" I usually tease them for a little while, but in the end I always tell them.

The truth is, though, when I get ready to say the seven words I always seem to feel the need to digress and first tell everyone what those seven words have come to mean to me and how they have changed my life. Then I get to telling stories I have heard or read about other people who have come to believe the same things, and it takes me awhile to say my seven words. In fact, I can usually use about as much time as the listeners will allow.

Even at the risk of your reading them and putting the book back on the counter, I am going to go ahead and tell you my seven words. Because if you begin to truly believe them, I will have said enough to you anyway. My words are: God has something to say to you!

Bob not only believed that the voice of God is in the Word of God but also believed that *we* are in that Word. He understood that it is a turning point in our relationship to the Bible when it becomes a "me book."

Recently in Nashville, a group of minister-marchers protested against the new paraphrase of the Scriptures called The Living Bible. *The polite name for them is "ultraconservative," a term which can also be roughly translated "redneck." Now you generally protest in Nashville in one of two places—the State Capitol or the Baptist Bookstore. Since there were no* Living *Bibles on sale at the Capitol, the logical place seemed to be the Baptist Bookstore. And so they came, and they marched.*

Now I don't doubt for an instant the sincerity of what they were trying to do. But I am convinced that if nobody ever goes down on Broad Street at the corner of Tenth across from the old Union Station and marches in front of the Baptist Bookstore, God is, and will be, speaking to people through His Word. No group of translators or scholars can lock God out of His own Word. He is alive, and He speaks through His Book.

The fact that we in the church treat God as if He were a wheelchair patient is utterly surprising. For instance, some people feel that God must be carefully protected and explained or He will not have enough life to make himself heard.

I certainly believe that as earlier and earlier manuscripts are found, men should carefully and diligently study and research to make every attempt to discover as nearly as possible the exact things God was saying through these men who wrote the Holy Bible. I am somewhere between amused and irked at all the people who feel that only through their eternal vigilance will God be able to speak through the Bible. If they are not careful, some group of translators will silence God forever.

This is the God-book. It is the speaking word of God, and His ability to speak through it does not depend on minister-marchers or involve hassles between various groups of fundamentalists on tenses and Greek and Hebrew words or on English words whose meanings have changed through history. It is the living, healing, moving, probing, convicting, speaking Word. And He has been, and He is, and He always will be heard through it, for it is filled with His life. It is the Living Word of God. It is the God-book.

But I am also convinced that His life makes it a "me book."

Out on the West Coast there is a company that has devised a very ingenious scheme for personalizing children's books. I'm sure the color illustrations throughout the book are printed in large mass runs for economy's sake. Then, on the basis of information the buyer sends along with the order, each book is run through a computer. Such questions as the child's name, age, birthday, street address, friends, dog or cat's name, and other assorted tidbits are put on the order blank. When the book is printed by the computer, each book is a story with the child as the chief character.

Last Christmas my mother ordered one of these books for our youngest son, Patrick. You can hardly imagine his surprise and delight when he pulled it out from under the tree and unwrapped it and began to read, "Once upon a time in a place called Hendersonville, there lived a little boy named Patrick Benson. Now Patrick wasn't just an ordinary little boy. This is a story about one of his adventures. It's the story of the day that Patrick met a giraffe . . ."

Over 70 times Patrick and his street and his friends were named, and when he got better acquainted with the giraffe it even had the same birthday and its name was "Kcirtap," which if you didn't notice is Patrick spelled backward.

Do you think Patrick likes that book? It is one of his favorite and most important books because to him it is a "me book." And I suspect we are all that way. We like stories about ourselves.

And this living book of God is about us. Read it—the King James, the Revised Standard Version, The New English Bible, The Living Bible, in the Greek or Hebrew, or any one of a dozen other translations, and you will find that He will be saying things to you that guide and comfort and bless and heal and answer the deep questions of your life.

We are in that book. It is a "me book" and a "you book." We all have taken our turn at saying, "There is no room in the inn," and we all know what it is like to sadly reverse our paths like the rich, young ruler. We all know what it is to say, "I do not know Him," or to leave unsaid, "Yes, I am a follower of His." We all have bravely said in stirring faith, "Thou art the Christ, the Son of the Living God," and we all have felt or said, "Unless I touch the nail prints on His hands."

It is not just a book written a long time ago about some people who lived way back then. It is about us. It is not just a book about a few men to whom He said, "Lo, I will never leave you." It is to us as well that these words still speak. Not only did He promise to turn their sorrow into joy, but He was saying to us just as surely as if He were looking us in the face that the thing that seems like sorrow to us today, He would have us writing poems and singing songs about tomorrow or next week. These things were said to us and for us and about us in this living Book of God.

Now, we all believe that, don't we? I haven't written any-

thing that we wouldn't all nod our heads in agreement on, have I? Then why don't, or why can't, we act like this is the Living Word. Why do we say, "I try to read the Bible, but it just is dull, monotonous, and routine?"

Maybe it is because we haven't realized that it is a "me book."

And that He not only was speaking to Paul on the Damascus road but also, just as surely, was speaking to Patrick on Bayshore Drive.

Because Bob believed that God would speak to those he loved through the Word he could relax and expect God to change lives.

I heard a man say the other day that he believed every word in the Bible was true. I certainly am not in disagreement with him, but on the other hand I am just as convinced that if and when God chooses to speak, He can and will even if somebody gets some of the words mixed up in the writing. Or in the preaching for that matter.

My son Tom recently asked me to buy him a new Bible. I guess you can't expect the Junior Department Graduation Bible to last for a lifetime. He said he wanted one with study aids and guides so he could find things. In the mood of a happy father, I began a search for a newer translation that had adequate helps for home study. When I found a Bible I thought would be satisfactory, I called him from the store and asked him if he would rather have the hardback or a leather binding. He said he wanted a "Bible-Bible," so I took the brown leather one home and gave it to him.

In a little while he brought it back and wanted me to inscribe it for him. So in the front I recorded the occasion—graduation from high school, the date, the recipient, and the givers. But over in the back where there were some blank pages for notes I wrote him a short letter. I reminded him that this was the book through which God speaks and if he would read its pages, God would surely speak to him. They might not necessarily be the exact same things that I have heard, but if he will read and listen, God would speak to him from those pages. And He will.

The temptation for me as a father, of course, is to somehow assume that it would be a lot better for me to tell Tom what God wants to say to him. That maybe if I don't explain what God is saying He will not be understood. I am slowly learning and although I deliver His message with all the earnestness I can, it is still secondhand. And it will only be life-changing when it comes firsthand.

The most important thing we can tell our children is that God will speak to them. Only when they have believed this, is it time to tell them what He told us.

And so Bob kept searching the Word for a word—a word that he might have missed or misunderstood—that might be the key to some treasure that God wanted to give him.

I am beginning to believe that He is always trying to say something good to me through the Scriptures. Even when He is commanding, I think if I could understand what He meant, I would find it is always something weighted with possibilities, surrounded by joy, and rooted in peace. All for me, all from Him.

And should *is the way I hear Him speaking to me.* Ought *and* must *speak with tones of enforcement, like "This is what will happen if you don't."* Should *seems to suggest more what will come to me if I do. And His voice does not ever seem to come to me in some sort of veiled threat, "If you don't . . ." It always seems to be coming to me as a gracious, gentle invitation, "If you do . . ."*

So I think He is saying something very rich to us when He says, "A man should lay down his life."

One of the things I hear Him saying here is that it is in laying down one's life that joy comes to us.

In this place He is using a trilogy of words. The first of the three is "joy" and the second is "love." These two words are certainly compatible, and it is not hard to think of them together. One would imagine that the third word in the trilogy would be "peace" or "hope" or "grace" or "mercy," or any of those other words we usually associate with happiness. But he is joining "joy" and "love" and "death." He is saying that joy and love and laying down our lives are three ideas that just naturally belong together. They are not mutually exclusive, like somebody said about the words "military intelligence." They are friends, and they travel hand-in-hand.

I am beginning to understand this a little bit. At the company I had a very good secretary. One of the things about an efficient secretary is that she keeps posted in your calendar, and hers, all the dates and appointments that are important. Each year she would mark my new calendar book with days I wanted to remember, like birthdays and anniversaries. A few days before the day, Karen would begin reminding me that I should buy a gift and a card.

Sometimes, I was especially busy and each day she would remind me again, and I would tell her that I had not forgotten. But when the day came and she asked me if I had been shopping yet, I had to say no. She knew the appointments for the day and knew that I would be busy all day long with one person or meeting after another, straight through lunch. In fact, by the time I would finish, it would be past time to get home for dinner. So she would say, "Do you want me to buy the present?"

"Well, yeah," I would weakly reply.

Did you ever give your wife an anniversary present that your secretary had bought? Well, it wasn't much fun to give, and I suspect it wasn't much fun to receive, either, because all of the giver that was involved were some dirty green pieces of paper. And no matter how many of them it took, it still did not represent as much as it should have, because it did not have the giv-

98

er's time, his love, or his thoughts. It only took me once to see that. There isn't much joy in giving what somebody buys and wraps for you.

When Jesus says, "A man should lay down his life," I believe that what He is trying to get us to see is that this is where joy and love are found. Not just for the receiver but for the giver as well. He is reminding us to release our gifts and graces and let them flow out of us and into others, knowing that as we do, joy and love will come flowing back to us.

Words such as "daily bread"—which we have lost through familiarity—could come alive again with Bob's touch.

Jesus talked about daily bread. When I read His words, I always find myself looking for deeper meanings. I always have the feeling that there was more to what He said than what I have seen. Here the disciples had asked Him to teach them to pray. So He gives them this prayer. It is lovely and meaningful. It has been memorized, carved into stone, and set to music from the earliest days of the church. It should be, because it came from His lips.

Still I wonder why He chose the ideas and petitions He did for this prayer. I am sure that each phrase has rich significance. So I wonder why He mentions daily. We're all so busy earning our daily bread that the least He could have done was to let us condense the petition time to weekly. What is He saying? What are those words trying to reveal to us?

They suggest to me that the graces and strengths of God are imparted to us a day at a time. Like the children in the wilderness, we need to learn that the manna is daily. Life is meant to be broken down into manageable parts. We are not to live our lifetimes, or the times of our lives, in union with Him, but we are to live our daily bread in union with Him.

Today may be our lifetime. Today is what we have. We must not waste its time or its moments in the anticipation of tomorrow.

I know there are values and necessities of preparation for the tasks and demands of a lifetime. I certainly believe in making plans for educating our children, for weddings, for retirement, and all the other issues that will confront us. But none of these are places where we will begin to live. We live now, today, and Jesus is saying, "Pray for this moment. This is the one."

No one captures all the dimensions of a story from the Bible quite like Bob Benson. Word by word, phrase by phrase he puts himself and us into the place where Jesus was. We are seeing the Savior, hearing Him . . .

The story begins very early on Easter Sunday at the tomb of Jesus in Jerusalem. It ends some seven miles away in Emmaus.

Mary Magdalene, Joanna, Mary, the mother of James, and some other women took spices they had prepared to the place where Jesus was buried. When they got there, the stone was rolled aside from the entrance. They went inside and found the body gone. They were standing there, utterly at a loss, when two men in bright and shining garments appeared beside them. In the women's terror, one of the men reminded them of Jesus' words about His death and resurrection.

Then the group of women began to recall what He had said and went to find the Eleven and all the others and tell them what had happened. But nobody would believe them. Later that day two of the men set out on their way to the village of Emmaus. Of course, they were talking about all that had happened in Jerusalem that week and Jesus came and walked along with them. But they didn't recognize Him.

It has always interested me that they did not know who He was. More than that, though, it has always intrigued me that He did not tell them. I have always wondered why He didn't rush up to them exclaiming, "It's Me! It's Me! It's over! I'm back! We won! It's Me! It's Me!"

The thing I am beginning to see is that it seemed more important for Him to wait until they said, "It's You! It's You!"

I think I can imagine a little of what Jesus must have been trying to do. It must be like encouraging your infant son to take his first steps. With open arms you wait. "Come on, come to Daddy. Let go of Mommy's hand and come to me."

You almost lean over and take his hand and pull him across the space that separates you. But that would not be walking. That would be pulling, wouldn't it? Walking is when he takes a step all by himself.

So I think Jesus is leaning as far as He can and still allowing them to come to Him in faith. He reminds them of the things Moses and all the prophets had written about Him. Surely, now they know. Hint after hint, clue after clue, until there was hardly anything left to say except, "It's Me! It's Me!"

But still nobody said, "It's You."

The sun had begun to drop in the west when they reached the village, but still they had not uttered the words of recognition. And now their roads must part. They were going home. He was going on. It was now or never. What should He do? Should He tell them now, or should He wait for another time and another place?

I believe that Jesus' heart jumped within Him when one of the men asked Him to stay for supper and the night. Time, a little more time for them to take the first faltering steps of faith.

It was one of those evenings when Father brings home an unexpected guest. Then Mother straightens the extra bedroom and apologizes for the supper. The kids are on their best behavior, having been reminded in the kitchen to mind their manners. They gather at the table. They ask Jesus to return thanks. They aren't sure who He is, but He must be religious because He knows all that Scripture.

He takes the bread and says the blessing. And then He breaks it and passes it down the table to each of them. And they say, "It's You!"

And He is gone from them.

I think I know what happened at the supper table that night. I can imagine what made them suddenly know who had walked with them all the way and was now at the table with them.

In a family the size of ours, it is hard to get everybody to the table on time. Somebody's always hollering, "Just a minute," back down the stairs. And it always takes longer than a minute. And then somebody else gets there a little early and helps Peg put the food on the table. They put everything but the broccoli, maybe, where they can reach it from where they sit. They even corral the salt and pepper and the butter. Although it's against the rules, occasionally someone even butters his bread before the rest of us get there. I am reluctant to admit it, but I have had to call on someone to return thanks who had to pray for food of which we were about to partake as well as some that was in the process of being partaken. It's hard to pray with a hot roll in your mouth.

Finally, though, the minute is up and we are all there. We join hands and say together: "Happy is he whose help and hope is in the Lord his God. Who keeps faith forever and gives food to the hungry. Praise the Lord. Amen."

So now I'm down at the daddy's end, and the food is somewhere clustered around the one who brought it to the table.

"Please pass the potatoes."

"Please pass the tomatoes."

"Please pass the meat."

"Please pass the salt." (You would think people would pass the pepper, too, when you asked for the salt, wouldn't you?)

"Please pass the butter."

And by now you are beginning to get some indication that they really wish you would stop bothering them so they could eat. You don't have any bread, but by now you decide you'll just put the butter on the potatoes and forget it. And then somebody, usually Peg, says, "Daddy doesn't have any bread. Someone pass Daddy the bread."

I'm believing that the thing that brought forth the glad recognition that night in Emmaus was just this. Jesus said,

"Cleopas doesn't have any bread. Somebody pass Cleopas the bread."

And Cleopas said, "It's You! It's You!"

We can study and discuss what Jesus came to do for humankind. We can learn all the prophecies about Jesus and give our assent to them. They can even become our creeds and beliefs. But it is when we realize that He knows we do not have any bread, and that He is starting it down the table to us, that we suddenly know who He is. He has been with us in our journey. He has been there all the time. He is with us.

Only such times of experience, only such moments can bring validity to religion. If we can hear His voice, we do not need any other proof. And if we cannot, then no other proof will do.

Of course, there are reasons for believing in God. Theologians and thinkers have gathered them up for us and distilled them into a few classical arguments. The order and purpose of the universe certainly tell us that there must have been a Designer. And both the matter and the motion of the universe point to the conclusion that there was ultimately a first cause. And the very fact that always there have been those who have believed there was a God indicates there is One. Where else would the idea have come from? And we recognize evil because we somehow perceive the good, and those perceptions bring us to an absolute good or truth.

But to understand or repeat any one of these beliefs or, indeed, all of them together, is not enough. Even if you know their big-word names—"cosmological," "teleological," "ontological," or whatever—they are inadequate. When life caves in, you do not need reasons, you need comfort. You do not need some answers, you need someone. And Jesus does not come to us with an explanation; He comes to us with His presence.

We are always seeking the reason. We want to know why. Like Job, we finally want God to tell us just what is going on. Why do the good die young and the bad seem to live on forever? If the meek inherit the earth, why do the arrogant always seem to have the mineral rights?

But God does not reveal His plan, He reveals himself. He comes to us as warmth when we are cold, fellowship when we are alone, strength when we are weak, peace when we are troubled, courage when we are afraid, songs when we are sad, and bread when we are hungry.

He is with us on our journeys. He is there when we are home. He sits with us at our table. He knows about funerals and weddings and commencements and hospitals and jails and un-employment and labor and laughter and rest and tears. He knows because He is with us. He comes to us again and again.

Waiting for us to say, "It's You! It's You!"

———◆———

It began to happen within the first few weeks of my acceptance of my first pastoral assignment. I received the calls almost every week for the next three years. They always began the same way.

"Good morning, Pastor. It's your dad."

What a lift on a Monday morning. Dad seemed to know how to tap into my situation by the words of greeting he offered me. A young pastor who, more often than not, was experiencing a blue Monday and who desperately wanted to be a shepherd but had suffered the numbing effect of low attendance or poor performance or little income to meet larger expenses.

"Pastor," he would say. And suddenly I felt like I belonged to that great tradition of men and women, called by the Master, to share His incarnational ministry. He knew, maybe better than many, what would put rise in my step and stiffness to my posture.

—*Michael W. Benson*

———◆———

8

WHO'S GOT THE URN?

Except for the years when he was pastoring, Bob Benson spent his entire life in one congregation. His grandparents had been part of a group of people from various denominations who had come together to form the Pentecostal Mission in Nashville. That Mission later became First Church of the Nazarene. Bob's father directed the music there for years. His roots were in that place.

Bob's books are peopled with the folks from First Nazarene.

There is a lady in our church, and I am ashamed to confess that I only know a few things about her. First, her name is Rose and her face always seems to be tinged with just a little sadness and struggle. Second, she always sits on the right side of the middle section on the first or second pew. Third, every time there is a call for prayer or an invitation song or a concluding song, Rose goes to the altar to pray. That's all I really know about her.

Peg and I were wondering one day about how the Lamb's Book of Life would look if it depended on Rose's faith and trust. Her name would be on every page an average of three times. It would look like this: Sam, Richard, Wilhemina, Rose, Charles, Alice, John, Mary, Rose, Pauline, Tracey, Keith, Lucas, Rose.

I can just hear some minor official saying, "Who is this Rose?"

I'll tell you one thing I would like to see. It may be some morning at the church. I surely hope that it isn't on one of the weekends that I have retreated somewhere. It may be when Rose gets to the Gate. Wherever it is, I would like to be there to see her face break into a smile that would eclipse a sunrise on a summer morning when she finally hears for the first time, "Rose, you are all right. You are OK. Everything is fine. You are complete."

From his life in that congregation, Bob remembered events and fashioned meanings that are his greatest legacy to us.

Do you remember when they had old-fashioned Sunday School picnics? I do. As I recall, it was back in the "olden days," as my kids would say, back before they had air conditioning.

They said, "We'll all meet at Sycamore Lodge in Shelby Park at 4:30 on Saturday. You bring your supper, and we'll furnish the iced tea."

But if you were like me, you came home at the last minute. When you got ready to pack your picnic, all you could find in the refrigerator was one dried up piece of bologna and just enough mustard in the bottom of the jar so that you got it all over your knuckles trying to get to it. And just two slices of stale bread to go with it. So you made your bologna sandwich and wrapped it in an old brown bag and went to the picnic.

When it came time to eat, you sat at the end of a table and spread out your sandwich. But the folks who sat next to you brought a feast. The lady was a good cook, and she had worked hard all day to get ready for the picnic. And she had fried chicken and baked beans and potato salad and homemade rolls and sliced tomatoes and pickles and olives and celery. And two big home-made chocolate pies to top it off. That's what they spread out there next to you while you sat with your bologna sandwich.

But they said to you, "Why don't we just put it all together?"

"No, I couldn't do that. I couldn't even think of it," you murmured in embarrassment, with one eye on the chicken.

"Oh, come on, there's plenty of chicken and plenty of pie and plenty of everything. And we just love bologna sandwiches. Let's just put it all together."

And so you did and there you sat, eating like a king when you came like a pauper.

One day, it dawned on me that God had been saying just that sort of thing to me. "Why don't you take what you have and what you are, and I will take what I have and what I am, and we'll share it together." I began to see that when I put what I had and was and am and hope to be with what He is, I had stumbled upon the bargain of a lifetime.

I get to thinking sometimes, thinking of me sharing with God. When I think of how little I bring, and how much He brings and invites me to share, I know that I should be shouting to the housetops, but I am so filled with awe and wonder that I can hardly speak. I know that I don't have enough love or faith or grace or mercy or wisdom, but He does. He has all of those things in abundance, and He says, "Let's just put it all together."

"Consecration," "denial," "sacrifice," "commitment," and "crosses" were all kind of hard words to me, until I saw them in the light of sharing. It isn't just a case of me kicking in what I have because God is the biggest kid in the neighborhood and He wants it all for himself. He is saying, "Everything that I possess is available to you. Everything that I am and can be to a person, I will be to you."

When I think about it like that, it really amuses me to see somebody running along through life hanging on to that dumb bag with that stale bologna sandwich in it saying, "God's not going to get my sandwich! No, sirree, this is mine!" Did you ever see anybody like that—so needy—just about half-starved to death yet hanging on for dear life. It's not that God needs your sandwich. The fact is, you need His chicken.

Well, go ahead—eat your bologna sandwich, as long as you can. But when you can't stand its tastelessness or drabness any

109

longer; when you get so tired of running your own life by your-self and doing it your way and figuring out all the answers with no one to help; when trying to accumulate, hold, grasp, and keep everything together in your own strength gets to be too big a load; when you begin to realize that by yourself you're never go-ing to be able to fulfill your dreams, I hope you'll remember that it doesn't have to be that way.

You have been invited to something better, you know. You have been invited to share in the very being of God.

One of the great examples that Bob has left for us is that he could be tied to one place by such bonds of the Spirit and yet be so free in his fellowship with people from other parts of the Body of Christ. Our unity in Christ was in Bob's heart. He *belonged* wherever God sent him, and his heart was to help others experience that oneness.

Bill Gaither and I were sitting on the edge of the darkened stage as the second Praise Gathering for Believers was about to begin. Over 6,000 people were in the audience. Even with the lights from the exit signs, the auditorium was almost totally black.

From the back of the auditorium, Doug Oldham began to sing. The people quieted down to hear Doug's warm voice as he slowly sang his way toward the front. About halfway down the aisle the spotlights caught him. He stopped and, in the midst of the expectant throng, he continued to sing.

When Doug finished singing he was going to introduce Bill and me. We were to welcome everyone to Indianapolis for what we hoped and prayed would be three days of life-changing wor-ship and praise. Neither of us was too certain about what he was going to say, and each of us was graciously deferring to the other.

Doug finished and gave us the microphone, and the spot-lights were on us. We began to try to welcome the people. We were just having some fun with the audience when I remembered something I had seen Chico Holliday do at a great evening of music in California a few months earlier.

I asked the people to identify themselves. "All the Methodists, say 'Methodist' together." Then I called, in turn, for Baptists, Presbyterians, Lutherans, Nazarenes, Church of Goders, Pentecostals, and on down through a list of all the groups that I could call to mind.

Then I asked everyone to call out the name of his or her group at the same time. On a signal everyone identified his church. It came out something like Baptodistyrianazaluther- anevepenschurchofgod.

Some groups are a little more active in their worship and they sounded out the strongest. But apparently some people from the more reserved groups had gotten some practice at basketball games or somewhere. They were not to be outdone. It was one more confusing sound of Babel.

After the confusion died down, I asked the audience to say "Jesus." When we spoke His name together there was such a unity that you could hardly believe the beauty. Bill said, "Let's whisper it together." That was the prettiest sound I think that I have ever heard. "Jesus."

Jesus is the name that unites us and make us one. When we all speak at once the names of the doctrines that divide us, it comes out in a word that nobody understands. We create a sort of religious shouting and shoving match. Hardly anyone other than the shouters and shovers is interested in the contest.

When we say His name together we make a beautiful sound that becomes "music in our ears, the sweetest name on earth."

Now, we don't all say the name of Jesus the same way. On almost back-to-back programs on the radio, you hear various preachers say "Jesus." They each say His name in such a different way that you wonder if they are all saying the same word. Some have perfected a pronunciation that comes out smoothly like "Je-suzz." Isn't that lovely? Just hang on the "suzzz." "Je-suzzz." It makes Him sound so warm and sweet.

The next program is hosted by some good old-time preacher

111

who is proclaiming the gospel as if he were fighting bees. He makes the name of Jesus a three-syllable word as he shouts, "Je-sus-aahh!" with great, moist emphasis on the "aahh!"

But regardless of how we speak the name of Jesus, it is the word that must be spoken. It is the one name that, when lifted up, draws all men in the same direction.

In Bob's study there was a big brass urn. I had enjoyed it and Bob's story that went along with it long before I knew where it came from. Not long after Bob's death I met a wonderful Christian brother whose name is Al Jaynes. Al's life is a living testimony to the unity of the Body of Christ. Bob's tale of what happens when we forget that the secret is in us was such a favorite of Al's that he bought the big urn and had it engraved "YOU'VE GOT THE URN."

At times there is a distinct advantage to being a slow reader. If you were just reading the important words you would be seeing "Christ," "hope," "glory," "he," and "proclaim." But bumping along from word to word, I dropped into the hole between "Christ" and "hope" and fell on two tremendous words: "in you."

Where is the secret? Where can you go to find it? Is it bigger than a breadbox? Tell me, where is it hidden? In you and in me. In common, ordinary, everyday folks like us.

Had I been God, I don't think I would have done that. I don't think I would have put the secret in us. I'm certain there are some of you who couldn't be trusted with such important matters. Of course, I trust me and I know that you would certainly do the same. After all, I am a published author. But there are really some strange folks around. I am trying not to think of anyone in particular, but I don't believe I would have included everyone.

Some people don't know how to keep a secret. Peg thinks a

secret is something that you tell one person at a time. That's not the worst of it. Some people can't even tell a secret. I heard of a lady who was passing on some very interesting and sensitive news to another lady. The listener was quite intrigued and wanted to know more. "I can't tell you any more," the first lady replied. "I've already told you more than I heard."

Some of us are just not too great at keeping secrets. We don't really lie. We're just like my son Tom—we remember big. But, despite all our inadequacies, we are the hiding places for the ultimate secret of the universe.

Could I use a word here about God that doesn't quite seem to fit, and yet it does? Would you let me say we have a "cool" God? Not "cool" like in cold or indifferent, but "cool" like He is confident in the way things are going to turn out.

I'm not so certain that all of His confidence was placed in us. I am certain that He was sure about the secret. He took that truth and put it within us. He had such confidence in the truth that He thought it would all end like He wanted it to. Most of us would have taken some kind of precaution to make sure it went the way we meant for it to go, wouldn't we?

Sometimes in my imagination I wonder what would have happened if He had appointed a committee from my church board to pick a place for the secret. I can just hear someone saying, "Let's get a great big golden urn and engrave the secret on it. Then if anyone wanted to read it, we'll all know right where it is. If we engrave an urn, no one can tamper with the wording. Since God speaks English, we'll putteth it in a beautiful old English script, something likened unto the King James Version."

I have observed the human predicament for a while, and I think I know what would have happened.

Seven or eight blocks from our old office, there is a huge building complex. It is the headquarters of the Baptist Sunday School Board. These buildings, along with one other over on James Robertson Parkway, are the headquarters for most of the departments that serve over 12 million Southern Baptists. With that many of them around, I want to be careful what I say.

The buildings cover areas of several blocks and are joined by walkways over the streets. There are entrances on Ninth Avenue, Tenth Avenue, Broad Street, Church Street, and probably some others I don't even know about. Security must be a problem.

If you wish to see someone in the headquarters complex, you have to state your business, and whom you wish to see, in the lobby before security will give you a badge to proceed. Then they will call ahead and warn the person that you are on your way. If they are the protectors of my good friend, Bill Reynolds, can you imagine what they might do if they had "the secret" in a big, golden urn in some room high atop the eighth floor?

"Good morning. My name is Bob Benson and I want to go up and see the urn and read the secret."

"That's fine, Mr. 'Vinson.' Could I see your card?"

Since I travel a lot I have all kinds of cards. I pull out my wallet and show them that I am in the Number One Club. I also have an Inner Circle card, which assures me of a hotel room with a window that overlooks the kitchen vents.

But they say to me: "Mr. Vinson, we mean your Southern Baptist Card."

"No, it's 'Benson,' B-E-N-S-O-N. I am not a Southern Baptist. You see, I am a Nazarene. I wanted to read the 'secret,' so I came to see the urn."

"You don't understand, Mr. 'Vincent.' We don't just show that to anyone. The only possible time you might get a glimpse of it would be when we are moving it to Ridgecrest or Glorietta for one of our solemn assemblies. Even then it is quite heavily guarded."

Suppose that, faced with such a situation, I got together with a few of my most trusted friends at church. One night we disguised ourselves to look like Southern Baptists. You know, white shoes and all. We broke into the Ninth Avenue entrance of Southern Baptist Headquarters and ripped off the urn. We rushed to Kansas City to put it where it belonged in the first place. If it were at our headquarters, we could decide whether we thought Southern Baptists ought to see it or not.

*While we were going through St. Louis, a group of Luther-
ans who had dressed up like Nazarenes—black socks and everything—crowded us off the road and, before we could resist, had
just plain "stolen" the urn from us rightful owners.*

*I don't know how the word spread so quickly, but before
they could get across the city someone from the headquarters of
the United Pentecostal Church got a group together and instructed them to be very quiet. Everyone had to promise not to
raise their hands in the air. In fact, it would be easier if they all
kept them in their pockets unless they were actually driving the
getaway bus or carrying the urn.*

*To tell you the truth, I don't know where the urn is now.
Sooner or later it will turn up, I guess. Someone will put it in a
tower and build a fence around it and keep other people from seeing it. The tower will become a shrine and people will sell tickets
to it. You will be able to buy color slides or little gold towers at
the concession stand. Somebody will put an "I've been to the
tower" sign on your bumper in the parking lot.*

*Other people will build motels and wax museums and ham-
burger stands. You can spend your entire vacation right there.
Of course, there will be tours so that you can ride by the tower
like you can ride by Johnny Cash's house. But you still will not
know the secret because nobody will let you see the urn.*

*Maybe the committee would think that everyone should
hear the secret. "Obviously they can't all read it for themselves,
but we can carry it to them. Let's engrave it on a bronze tablet,
and we'll go all over the country and have big rallies and read
the secret to them.*

"Great! we can sing and praise the Lord."

"We can all raise both hands while we sing."

*At this point a great amount of discussion would take place
within the committee. Some would feel it would be better to raise
only one hand. Still others would be sure it would be much more
dignified to just sing without raising your hands at all.*

*The "two handers" quote from the Psalms about raising
your hands to the Lord. "See, it's plural," they insist. The "one*

handers" check into the Hebrew meaning of the words and argue very persuasively that when everybody raised one hand it would be plural collectively and this was the proper interpretation of the passage.

Finally, the matter of the order or "ardor" of the service surrounding the reading of the secret would be referred back to a subcommittee and the tour is delayed. For a while at least, the rallies won't be held and you won't be able to hear the "secret."

Some members of the committee don't even know yet—God told everybody. It is not somewhere you can't afford to go. It is not guarded by someone who won't let you see it. It is not the prized possession of some group or committee who will only give you access to the secret if you look, act, and dress in a certain way.

The secret is in you.

When we would drive to the Benson Company at Metro Center we would pass—high on a hill—St. Cecelia's Convent. I must admit that on more than one morning, when we were facing big deadlines, I considered turning in and joining up! Bob was always curious about the place and so he asked his lawyer, who was Catholic, about visiting. He made the arrangements and a wonderful friendship began.

Bob would visit and would give Vespers devotionals for the sisters there. Because his heart was so open he could cross theological, cultural, and gender barriers to know fellowship with these women.

When Bob was dying at St. Thomas Hospital the Mother Superior at St. Cecelia's was told of his illness. She sent the novices—lovely young women who sang like angels around Bob's bed. He knew that the secret was not in places. The secret was in people.

———————◆———————

Dad and Leigh and I set out to climb the Chimneys together. To be honest it was a struggle for Dad. People with asthma don't always make good mountain climbers, and Dad wasn't very strong to boot, and so it took us a while in the snow and ice. But we made it.

We didn't stay up there very long, since we had taken most of the afternoon light coming up and we were afraid to let it get too dark before we started back down. But there was time for an apple or two and a candy bar that we had saved for the occasion and so we sat for a few minutes together. Nobody said much; we all just kept grinning at each other. And we snapped what was left of a roll of film that I had, just in case we needed proof later on that we hadn't bailed out along the way.

A few weeks later, the next time I saw my dad, he had spoken for what was to be the last time, and he was about to check into the hospital for what was to be the last time too.

I took the pictures we had shot up on the mountain to show Dad one night not long after the doctors had gathered us all together to tell us that he wouldn't be coming home to us again. The doctors saw the pictures, too, and couldn't believe that he had even tried the climb much less finished it. I wasn't surprised much. He spent most of his life climbing up one mountain or another—illness, discouragement, rejection slips, business problems, and the stuff that goes with being a parent to five kids.

I could have told the doctors that my dad was always funny like that, he just thought mountains were for climbing. He also thought songs were for singing and hands were for holding and people were for loving and stories were for telling and life was for living. He may not have been here long, but he didn't miss much.

—**Robert Benson**
Hermitage, Tennessee
October 1, 1986

———————◆———————

9

THE FELLOWSHIP OF SUFFERING

The life that Bob Benson shared with his listeners was full of promise and possibility. He was active and creative and celebrative. He was also a patient. For a great deal of his life Bob was sick.

I worked with Bob. I traveled with him. I ministered with him. But the longest stretches of time I spent with him were in the hospital. I realize now that many of the deepest things I know about Bob came to me because of what can only be called *the fellowship of suffering*.

Trips to the beach are more fun to write about than trips to the doctor. Remembering Bob's philosophy is more inviting than recalling his chemotherapy. I always preferred watching him help to watching him hurt. But illness and pain were part of reality for Bob Benson. So they must be a part of his story.

Whenever I am tempted to draw back from the suffering of my friend I always recall that part of what made Bob so real for those who heard him and read him was that he told the whole story. He didn't leave out the part about his temper. His kids didn't always get the MY CHILD OUT-DID YOUR CHILD AT HENDERSONVILLE ELEMEN-TARY bumper stickers. He wasn't always chosen.

He wasn't always sick. But a lot of the time he was.

Bob played a better-than-average game of tennis. He

didn't need a handicapped tag for his car. But major illnesses turned his life upside down on several occasions.

My mother, who brought up five children, recently wrote in her memoirs that I was "the only baby she raised who had none of the normal baby ailments." She reported that I "ate what I was fed, digested it, slept well, and was generally happy and a delight." Someone has since pointed out that I was either resting up to be sick from then on, or else I was playing some kind of monstrous trick on my parents, not to mention myself. My dad, who is the family historian, recently said that as far as he was able to determine, I was certainly among the leading contenders for being the sickest of the clan in at least seven or eight generations.

By the time I was four, my brother John was beginning to bring home from school all the common childhood illnesses. In one year alone he spread measles, chicken pox, and mumps through our household. Early on I showed a marked talent for getting sick as soon as the two of them, John and the disease, came in the door. Generally, I was not one to mess around with a mild case either.

When I was six years old or so I came down with severe asthma. This new ability to develop my own diseases marked a turning point in my life. No longer would I have to wait for someone to bring them to me. Ever since that time I have shown a remarkable propensity to come up with illnesses and maladies that were new to the family.

Bronchial asthma is among the most serious of childhood diseases and afflictions. It is baffling and capricious and unlike other illnesses such as scarlet fever or getting your tonsils taken out. You do not just get over it. One never seems to know when another attack is to be forthcoming.

For reasons unknown, asthma is usually a disease of the night, often occurring in the wee hours of the morning. It begins with a tightening of the chest and a dry cough. Breathing be-

comes more and more difficult until one is panting for air. In fact, the Greek word for asthma is "panting." This is accompanied by a deep wheezing and one is forced to sit up in bed, battling, struggling, fighting for breath with elbows propped on knees, shoulders hunched, and head thrown back literally gasping for air. It is a terrifying experience for a small boy, and I suspect it must have been equally terrifying for my young parents.

Mom and Dad would come to me in the middle of the night with the usual treatments. There was the Asthma Nefrin nebulizer with the squeeze bulb that was good at dropping off and rolling under the bed. And there was a greenish powder called Asthmador, which you burned in a jar lid so you could inhale the smoke. I would pile it up like a tiny mountain and light it in one spot and watch the flaming sparks spread like a forest fire until it was blackened all over. Hopefully, the rising smoke allowed me enough breath to lie down again and go back to sleep. Asthmador also came in cigarettes and as a mixture for pipe smoking but, of course, I only read about these forms of evil on the side of the can.

On cold winter nights when an attack would come and I would be unable to breathe lying down, Dad would build a fire in the fireplace and tuck the covers around me in his big easy chair. Mom would read to me until I would finally fall asleep again. Sometimes, if the nebulizer or the smoke wouldn't work, they would bundle me up and take me over to Dr. Elliott's house on Eastdale Avenue for a shot of adrenaline.

Between attacks there were trips to all kinds of doctors and specialists with numerous tests to try to determine what was the cause. It was apparent that the fall of the year was the most difficult season for me, and the ragweed and other things in the air would give me attacks. I spent many weeks out of school and the homebound teacher would come to me. Sometimes my mother would take me to North Carolina to see if the mountain air would help. Sometimes we would go to Florida or the Alabama coast to see if the sea air was any freer of the pollens that provided the attacks. But usually something—dust, pollen, damp night air, changes in temperature, cat fur, dog hair, feather pillows, being at home, being away from home, or some culprit unknown to me—managed to continue to disrupt my life by provoking asthma to "attack" me.

Even when I was feeling well enough to go to school, there were many notes sent along to everybody about how to "take care of Bob." Of course, I was told always to keep my head covered, my sweater on, and my feet dry. Once I remember it started snowing one afternoon while we were in school. The class could hardly wait for the bell to ring so we could get out into the big, moist snowflakes that were already beginning to cover the ground. There was a knock on the seventh grade classroom door, and I saw a mother's hand pass a pair of galoshes through the crack in the doorway to the teacher. Being especially susceptible to such protection, I remember thinking how embarrassed some poor kid was going to be. And I can remember even clearer the feeling when Mrs. McDaniel turned to the class and said, "Bob Benson, come get your galoshes."

As you might well imagine, as a father now, I have a much deeper appreciation for my parents' investment in midnight vigils and trips to anywhere there might be help and galoshes when it began to snow during the school day.

I don't always know what to say about my illnesses. As much of the time as we can at our house, we try to laugh about them. Just the other morning Peg remarked that she had a cold and I responded, "I do too." She accused me of trying to have everything she did. So we decided to divide the diseases. She would have all the minor ones and I would have all the major stuff—the things that really bring out people's sympathy and flowers and cookies and cards. In the case of a brand-new disease, I am to get the first option until we find out whether or not it is going to be major.

But then again, I don't know what to say about my wellnesses, either. As surely as I do not understand why I so often have been the one to get sick, neither do I understand why I am the one who has so often gotten well from so many things. But I *do believe that something has grown out of both experiences over the years that has enriched the soil into which my faith has sunk its roots.*

There was some kind of lesson learned, however faint it might have been when I was younger. Maybe it was about vulnerability. To be sure, there were mornings when it was nice in a way to be staying home as John and Laura were getting ready for school. But there were other times when I could not help but wonder why I wasn't as sturdy as Bill Hunt or Roland Downing or Mack Parsons who always seemed ready to play in the woods and along in the creek that flowed through our backyard.

Early on, there was a dimly increasing awareness that all was not as it was purported to be. Then even though it seemed that most of life's lessons had to do with oneself—self-control, self-development, self-assertiveness, self-preservation—maybe there was something truer to be learned. Life was simple on the surface. One only had to learn to talk, walk, dress, read, write, add, subtract, multiply, divide, ride a bicycle, drive a car, and acquaint oneself with some important, but never again to be used, facts such as Boise is the capital of Idaho and water is two parts hydrogen and one part oxygen. One had to learn to make choices and to make waves and to make a living and then came the rewards—self-confidence, self-support, self-reliance, completeness.

It is a strong theory, but it doesn't always test out well when as a kid you wake up in the middle of the night unable to catch your breath. Or later on, in a sort of a midlife course correction, when a doctor tells you this particular lump is malignant and must be removed. One does not particularly become a theologian at 7 (or 42, either), but there has always seemed to be the sound of other meanings coming forth from somewhere back there—a sound that quietly but firmly pointed out that faith would have to find its refuge outside of self. That sound gently but resolutely confirmed that there was One who could gather up the circumstances of our days and use them to His purposes and to our good.

It is partially, at least, from this perspective of illness and wellness that I so strongly see and believe that one can come to know that God is infinitely willing and abundantly able to bring good out of the processes of our lives. Perhaps this is also where I have begun to learn to hear the calling voice of God in the happenings and events of life.

Bob's life taught me a lot about the *processes.*

Sometimes in retreat prayer times, I will ask people to envision a blank sheet of paper with a horizontal line across the middle. Then, giving them time for reflection, I ask them to remember the good things that have happened to them across the years, to think about them and rejoice over them. And I have them "write" those things one by one on the paper above the line. (I confess that I often "watch and pray" so that I may enjoy the looks of peace and pleasure on the faces in front of me.)

Then, to help them get a truer perspective of how God works in their lives, I also suggest they recall the evil things that have come to them as well, the deep troublesome times that threaten to engulf their souls. I ask them to "list" those below the line. And I watch the expressions of pain move across their faces as they recall things that have swept in on them with devastating suddenness and fury. I try to close these prayer times by reminding the audience that the whole paper can be committed to Him. He is the God of the list on the top and the God of the list on the bottom.

A very interesting thing always happens afterward. Sometimes just one person and sometimes several people will find me afterward just to talk. The places may vary, but the conversation is always the same, "You know, when we were listing those things on the paper in prayer, and we put that stuff above and below the line? There were some things that, for the life of me, I didn't know where to put. Even now I am not sure. Some of those things are so evil it would seem their place would be a foregone conclusion. The day they happened, I knew all right. The bottom of the bottom wasn't low enough. I didn't know whether I would make it or not. But now, looking back, I'm not so sure. Some of them seem to be creeping over the line."

In their eyes there usually is a depth that reveals a mixture of both joy and sorrow, both peace and pain. Their brows are often furrowed and many times their hair is gray. But they say to me, "I guess I have to write it above the line." Even out of the darkest circumstances His call to us can be heard.

More and more it seems that those of us who make up retreats are a microcosm of society in general. One has only to show a little bit of openness and willingness to listen, to be allowed into the worlds of hurt reflecting all of the ills of society. For we are, or carry the burdens of, the sick, the deranged, the illegitimate, the elderly, the divorced, the poor, the unloved, and the unwanted. We are all there. Almost anything that has happened anywhere has happened at some time to one of us.

I listen to people and my heart breaks for them. Sometimes I think I would like to put my arms around them and promise them that I will personally see that nothing else bad ever happens to them again. But I cannot even protect my own from the hurts of life. There are only about three things I know to say to them. The first is that I will pray for them.

Sometimes I think we just say that we will pray for someone because there doesn't seem to be anything we consider practical or helpful we can do, something like sit with the children or cook supper, or run some errands. So we say, "I'll pray for you." I am coming to believe that there is nothing more important that we can do for anyone than to pray for them. I confess to them that I am not so good at it, but I do have time, and I will pray for them and for their son or daughter or estranged husband or diseased body or perplexing situation.

I have found that offering to pray for someone often leads me to ask if there is anything else I can do. For we cannot let them into our hearts alone. Prayer is not an escape from the pain and reality of the world; rather it is a clearer, more compelling *awareness of it. And we are led to some other way in which we may be of help.*

The other thing that I always want to do is impart this truth—God is able to work in the darkest, direst set of circumstances. Many times, in light of the story just told me, it seems impertinent or even irreverent to suggest it. Still, on the basis of the gospel, and on the basis of my own experiences, I want to tell these people that I believe God will turn their sorrows into joy.

I know there are terrible and tragic things that befall people. There are wrongs that can never be righted again, events and misfortunes that are still as unfair and as bewildering years later as they were the dark night that they occurred. And even though it seems almost a sacrilege to say it to the broken, wounded person who stands weeping before me, I always find myself saying, "Someday you will sing about this very sorrow."

We may lay claim to the promises of God in a moment of profession. We may rest on them. We may trust them implicitly. We may live in accordance with the precepts and admonitions. We may read and memorize the words of Jesus and be certain that they are true. We may have no doubt that God will be with us always because He has promised us that He would. But somewhere on the journey, pain or sickness or sorrow will be ours. Our faith will belong to us.

Knowing His presence, knowing that He is indeed who He says He is, and knowing that He can do what He claims He can do becomes the truths that form His message to us. That message tells us "in all things" He is working for our good. And the joy of "knowing him" is the joy that transforms our sorrows.

I must admit that I do not even think of time spent with Bob in the hospital as bad time. I remember that during one weeks-long stay I would come every night between 10:00 and 11:00 to stay until morning. Our friend Morris Stocks had come earlier in the evening when it was time for Peggy to leave. Often Morris would be singing to Bob, and I would wait in the sitting room and listen.

Jesus! what a Friend for sinners!
Jesus! Lover of my soul!
Friends may fail me, foes assail me;
He, my Savior, makes me whole.

I know now that if Bob's illness had not brought us all to that hospital suite, Morris would have been busy at the college, I would have been immersed in things at the church, and Bob would have been retreating or advancing somewhere. But here we were together and that made the whole thing bearable.

I learned some lessons from the way Bob faced illness. I suppose it's not fair for him to have done the suffering and me to have gotten all this wisdom. I believe that there were three incredible things about the way he faced illness.

Bob faced illness with humor. I used to tell him when he would make wisecracks from his hospital bed that in a world of standup comics he was the original lay-down comic.

Once we were holding a retreat together in south Georgia. On Saturday night a crowd of us went into town and ate pizza and during the night Bob was very sick. By the time we got back to Nashville he had to be hospitalized. Ten days later he had radical colon surgery.

While we were waiting for the verdict on his surgery I was sitting with him one afternoon. He said, "Do you know 'I Left My Heart in San Francisco'?"

"I surely do," I responded.

"Well, how about 'I Left My Colon in Tifton, Georgia'?"

Several weeks later I was helping him walk the halls of the hospital to try to get his strength up so that he could go home. I was pushing the IV pole along when we passed a mirror and Bob got a good look at himself. In what could have been one of the least funny moments of life this man who would not let us stop laughing had one thing to say.

"I look like I traded legs with a jaybird and got beat out of my rear end in the deal."

Bob faced illness with humility. He often talked about

other people who were suffering in various ways and seemed to feel that he was no better than they to face life's hardships. He experienced the indignities of hospitalization and treatment without complaint. The only right he seemed to demand was to wear pajamas instead of a hospital gown. He thanked his caregivers. He thanked God—for every healing and for each day.

Bob faced illness with hope. Even after a dark prognosis he kept planning vacations and books and celebrations. He was booked to speak at retreats and conventions. He anticipated graduations and grandchildren. He seemed to have fully grasped Charles Spurgeon's belief that "A man is immortal until his work on earth is done."

The basis of Bob's hope was nothing other than the incarnation of Jesus—His presence in whatever life might bring.

Last Christmas was one of the brightest, happiest times I can remember. My heart is still filled with such delightful memories that I am smiling just thinking about it.

We had just moved into a new house. Well, it was new to us anyway. After 20 years in your other place, you wonder whether you will ever be able to feel at home in the new one.

Our old house had grown with the family over the years. Robert and Mike and I had remodeled the garage into a recreation room. Later, with the help of a real carpenter, we had added a dining room, primarily to display some stained-glass windows we found in a junk shop. The kitchen had been enlarged and a sunny plant room attached. Finally, a guesthouse with a place for a study for me was added until we sprawled across the hillside overlooking Old Hickory Lake. Now we had decided to move south, closer to town. We wondered, though, if we could ever find a place we would learn to love as well as our lakeside home.

When we drove by and saw the "For Sale" sign in the yard, we knew this faded brown New England saltbox with the yellow

*door was for us. With some paint and wallpaper, it has become
an almost perfect setting for Peg's antiques and primitives.*

*Sometimes, it seems like we've been moving to Birmingham
20 miles at a time because this was really our second move within the year. Rather, it was Peg's second move. I was in the hospital when the time came to leave the other house. So Peg and the
kids moved. But when I got out, I found them. She can't get
away from me. I've told her if she ever decided to leave me she
should pack my bags, too, because I am going with her.*

*The people from the church had helped pack, move, and put
everything away again in the condominium where we were going
to live until we could decide where to settle more permanently.
At least they helped her put away all you could squeeze from 11
rooms and guesthouse into a three-bedroom condominium. We
had a lot of stuff stored in friends' attics and basements all over
town. One of the reasons it was so good to get in the new house
was to unpack things that we hadn't seen in months. It was like
a housewarming shower all over again.*

*One of the things that we unpacked was the manger scene.
The figures are wooden carvings and they are complete, even
down to two, tiny sleeping roosters. On vacations over the years,
I have collected stones and pieces of driftwood from hikes and
woods and walks on beaches to make the stall and the manger
and the background. So setting up the crèche is my job. When I
first started, Peg thought it would be better if I did it in the play-
room. But I have gotten so good at it that this year she let me put
it in the living room on her new wicker coffee table top. It was
one of my better efforts, if I say so myself. And it seemed to speak
to all of us anytime we went into the living room. A couple of
nights we sat in front of the manger and listened to "The Messi-
ah." Once in a while I think we ought to set it up in June.*

*And all of the children were going to be here in our new
home for Christmas. Nothing can make a father of five any hap-
pier than to have them all home at once. Especially with the
bonus of daughters-in-law and a grandson. Leigh had gotten
home early in December. She had been there to help pick out the*

tree and to help her mother decorate the house and hang the wreaths on the doors. Tom and Patrick had given up their rooms to their older, married brothers and moved in on Leigh's sofa.

For once I had done my shopping early, but on Christmas Eve morning, Leigh and I made one last desperate trip just for old times' sake. When we got home at noon, the aroma of the turkey baking in the oven wafted through the house. I puttered around the house, but I was really keeping an eye on the driveway for the maroon VW convertible that was bringing Mike and Gwen home to us from Kansas City, where he is in his seminary program. The school where Gwen teaches music didn't get out until the afternoon of the 23rd, and they were driving halfway that night and the rest of the way on Christmas Eve.

Late in the afternoon Robert and Jetta were going to fly in from Chicago. He was planning to leave his marketing agency office a little early in time to pick Jetta up at the hospital where she is a medical technologist. And they would catch the plane that would bring them home to us.

After dinner we were all going to an eleven o'clock Christmas Eve candlelight service. The pastor and his family were out of town, and I had been asked to be in charge. Mike was going to read the Scripture, and some of my favorite friends were singing. All of my family would be seated in the first pew, and I knew I would be having the happy privilege of seeing their faces bathed in brightness as they each lit a Christmas candle.

Need I tell you that my heart was so full of happy anticipation and mingled memories that my feet were barely touching the floor?

Then, as if I didn't have enough to be happy about, a few days before, I had received some fine news from the surgeon. "No surgery in January." You don't know what this means to a coward. I had been too sick during the surgery back in the spring for them to complete what they had started out to do. Now he told me that a procedure was being perfected that might enable them to correct what they had begun. Not only was the surgery not going to be completed in January, but I could wait, and then maybe, the whole procedure could be reversed.

So as Christmas came to our house, I felt most wonderfully blest. Good health, good news, a large, loving family, a new home, and lots of friends to share it.

But it was not Christmas because the recent days had brought us to a new home. It was Christmas because Jesus brings us life. Not everybody had a new home. A young couple in our church, Rick and Jeanie, came home a few days before Christmas to find their apartment in flames and everything they owned gone.

It was not Christmas because all of the kids had come home. It was Christmas because Jesus has come. Some people didn't have their loved ones with them. The only sad part about Christmas this year was that Mom and Dad were far away in Florida where he was recuperating from a painful illness. It was the first time in years we hadn't all gone over to their house for Christmas morning breakfast, including freshly squeezed orange juice and homemade biscuits.

And it was not Christmas because I had good news from the doctor. It was Christmas because Jesus was born. Not everybody had good news from the doctor. Back in the summer when I was in the hospital for a short second trip, a friend received the same grim diagnoses the doctor had given me. We knew the whole family well. When I directed a teen group in our church, her kids, Ronnie and Becky, were in it. I learned to love them both. I had gone to school with her husband, Paul. She was buried a few days before Christmas.

Still, it was Christmas at the Langfords'; it was Christmas at the folks' in Fort Myers; it was Christmas at the Shields'. It was Christmas because Jesus is born. There is no Christmas without Him. All the rest is just tinsel on the tree.

And the same is true with all of the rituals and all the events of our lives: Thanksgivings, birthdays, commencements, funerals, weddings, and all the others are tied just as inexorably to Him. He is the very center of all the days of our lives. These words Jesus uses are pointed, but they are true: "Apart from me . . . nothing."

He is not saying that He is the life of the Christian, although that is true. He is not saying that He is the life of the church, although He is.

He is saying that His is the Life of life.

The idea hit him on our family trip to Europe. Bob planned a vacation for all of our family—which included our own children and spouses plus Bob's parents who were in their 70s at the time. He was concerned that in all the noise and confusion of our travels through large airports, our younger boys, who were 8 and 10, might wander off and be lost. When we arrived at London's Heathrow airport, an idea began to take shape.

All around us were tour groups being met by very official looking leaders that carried tall signs over their heads with the name of their groups displayed. Bob, who never was at a loss to capitalize on an idea, decided if they could have a sign so could he. And so he did—his sign was his long "crookneck" umbrella and he decided right then and there when he wanted to find us, or get our attention or change the plan—all he would have to do was raise that umbrella high over his head. Our job was to watch for it. It was our signal to check in with daddy, who wanted to make sure we were all right and that we understood the plan.

Often I like to imagine Bob in heaven and what he might be doing. Once I read that Peter Marshall said he thought heaven might be getting to do some things you always longed to do on earth, but never had the proper time. Peter said, for him, that might be to grow lovely hybrid roses. He was sure they would have a heavenly fragrance and that there wouldn't be an insect in sight. That always sounded like a good idea to Bob too. He liked the thought of an eternal blooming garden or maybe even finally having time to lie in a hammock and just drink in the heavenly view. Often when I'm flying I imagine him running through the clouds raising his arms in grateful praise to his Heavenly Father. But I guess the way I picture him most is over in one corner, scanning the crowd looking for his loved ones, and over his head he holds his tall crookneck umbrella.

—Peggy Benson

10

HOME AT LAST

If Bob Benson had lived to know all his grandchildren, he would have had a million more stories. They are forever doing and saying the kinds of things that he used to turn on the lights inside people's minds and spirits.

Just this past Fourth of July, Lacy and Grant, Tom's two, had a busy weekend planned with the cousins. Dad was taking them to a picnic in the country at Britt and Annie's. Then there came a second invitation—to go to the wave pool with Uncle Robert and Jettabeth and Jeffrey.

Grant and his sister were fishing with their dad, and Grant was struggling with the picnic/wave pool decision.

"Dad, should we go to the wave pool?" he asked.

Tom decided it was time to test his dad's theories on nondirective parenting.

"Well, Grant, I don't know. It would mean you would miss the picnic at Aunt Leigh's."

Grant thought. Grant studied. Finally Grant seemed to have hit on something. He picked up two rocks and showed them to Tom.

"I've got it, Dad."

"You do?" Tom said.

"This rock is the wave pool, and this one is the picnic. I am going to throw them into the water. The one that goes the farthest is the one that I'll do."

With that he hurled the wave pool rock into the lake with all the might that a nine-year-old arm could muster. And then, with measured nonchalance, he dropped the picnic rock just in front of him.

"Guess it's the wave pool, Dad."

Bob would have helped Grant teach us all about how we tilt God's will in the direction we want to go. He would have listened to the truth of this new generation, and he would have helped that truth along.

One morning Grant was getting ready for school. He combed his hair especially slick and then turned to his grandmother.

"Gram, do you think he would have liked me?"

"What, Grant?" Peggy responded.

"Papa, Gram. Do you think he would have liked me?"

"Yes, Grant. He would have liked you a lot."

If Grant could have known his papa, he would have had no doubt that he liked him. Love was no guessing game for Bob Benson.

When Bob went to the hospital for the last time, he was weak and weary from battling cancer. No more surgery. No more chemotherapy. Just waiting.

Peggy and I were talking about how little strength he had left. I reminded her that everyone thought he or she was Bob's best friend. He had his wife, his mother, five children, four brothers and sisters—all of whom needed to be with him. She would have to draw a "Family only" line, and we would all have to honor it.

But one day, after I thought I had seen him for the last time, Peggy told me I should go in to see him. And so I did.

It was not a happy time in my life. My friend was dying. I was a principal who really wanted to be a teacher. I was sad.

When I sat down beside Bob's bed, his eyes were closed. After a few minutes I leaned over him and called his name. He opened his eyes. Then he gave me one of the most precious gifts of my life.

With his bony hands he cupped my not-so-bony cheeks. That soft voice—now even softer—said, "That face, that face. I love that face."

A few days later Bob Benson died.

There were so many other faces that Bob loved. Each of them has memories of his or her walk with him. I have written this simple remembrance for the faces he never saw. But he would have liked—he would have loved—those faces. They would have liked him and listened to him. And they would never have been the same.